MOMENTUM

4 March 1990

To Graydon, Jennie, Amber, and Josh :
Thank you for your kind hospitality
and warm fellowship.

— Wallace Alcorn

MOMENTUM

WALLACE ALCORN

LIVING STUDIES
Tyndale House Publishers, Inc.
Wheaton, Illinois

Unless otherwise noted, all Scripture references
are from the *Holy Bible, New International Version;*
Copyright © 1978 by New York International Bible
Society. Other quotations are from the *Revised
Standard Version of the Bible* © 1946, 1952 by
Division of Christian Education of the National
Council of the Churches of Christ in the United
States of America and from the King James
Version of the Bible.

First printing, April 1986
Library of Congress Catalog Card Number 85-52098
ISBN 0-8423-4538-8
Copyright © 1986 by Wallace Alcorn
Printed in the United States of America

CONTENTS

FOREWORD

This book comes not only from the Bible and the Holy Spirit, but some of God's people have had a part in producing it. I am deeply grateful to those who helped me learn by learning with me.

I think first of the congregation of Milwaukee's Garfield Baptist Church and their spiritual leader, Pastor Edward Fuller. They gave me the opportunity of working through with them the warnings and exhortations in the Epistle to the Hebrews in a Fall Bible Conference. That got me started on the book.

A tour of active duty as a training developer at the United States Army Chaplain Center and School at Fort Monmouth, New Jersey, gave the opportunity of testing the material again. Through private conversations with students in both the Basic Course and Advanced Course and through preaching in the School's chapel services, I learned to strengthen reasoning and sharpen expressions.

I should be pleased if all these would feel in this book some sense of contribution. Regardless, you did encourage me. Thank you.

PREFACE

In preparation for reading the expositions here, I recommend you read through each text in the New International Version of the Bible given at the head of each chapter.

Some of the Bible quotations within the chapters are in language that resulted from my own exegesis of the Greek text, not to compete with the published versions, but simply to express the meaning in terms of the immediate study.

At times my translation may tend to be more paraphrastic than the standard versions. My purpose is to draw out and highlight the specific aspect of the text we discuss. For a full paraphrase, however, you do well to turn to *The Living Bible* or *The New Testament in Modern English* (J.B. Phillips).

I respect the fact that many readers are most familiar with the King James Version (KJV, 1611); and its language is as firmly fixed in their minds as the Scripture it communicates is in their hearts. Reading the New International Version of the Bible and considering these translations will, I hope, give fresh perspective to the understanding of the Word of God.

So, too, have I given the treatment of the Revised Standard Version (RSV) for those who use it as their regular version. I have also made some attemjpt to display the textual evidence upon which some of my interpretations are based. The reader should be aware that there is much more evidence and argumentation behind my conclusions than he will read here.

For more of my thinking on the Epistle to the Hebrews itself, I refer to my article on the book in *The Wycliffe Bible Encyclopedia*.

ONE
DON'T FALL BACK, OR YOU'LL DROP OUT

God promises his children so much, but most of us have so little. Salvation from sin is great, yet we often seem unable to escape sin. The Christian life is supposed to be thrilling, but for some, it seems to be such a drag!

We don't admit it, but our lives betray the fact that there is no joy. Nothing seems real.

Knowing others also face this problem helps, yet it doesn't solve the problem. The condition persists and it refuses comfort.

There is help! Christians in the past have felt the way many of us do now, and then went on from there. Not only did that considerable number feel better, they actually received what God promised and went on to lives that satisfied themselves, enriched others, and pleased God.

This book tells about those people, and it tells how any of us can have the same experience. There is no limit to what our Christian experience can become.

Don't be suspicious. There is no secret about to be revealed that has been hidden from Christians through the ages. It's no wild scheme, which never worked for anyone. And I am not promoting one more cult, which keeps people so busy they don't notice that they have only substituted one illusion for another.

Another Bible study book? No. I truly hope readers will study the Bible as a result of this, but that's not what I'm asking now.

The Epistle to the Hebrews offers the sort of thing we need. It took me a while to realize this because Hebrews once seemed such a weird book that I passed over to easier things.

Hebrews is a unique book. It uses some strange illustrations and explanations. Yet once we get the feel, it speaks with a wisdom heard nowhere else. Hebrews is encouraging. It is one grand encouragement to live a successful spiritual life—which is altogether possible.

It changed my life. In fact, I don't think it too much to say Hebrews has given me life. I had realized what little value religion has for me even though, as a nonliturgical evangelical, I had thought I was rather free of religion. It dawned on me that religion really was holding me back from spiritual experience.

As I dropped religious mechanics, I picked up some specific spiritual things I could do. The alternative to religious busyness, I learned from this book, is not pious idleness, but the exciting experience of really living.

DANGEROUS CONDITIONS OF THE CHRISTIAN LIFE

Hebrews' exhortations encourage Christian believers to a growing, wholesome spiritual life. Spiritual health and strength is the goal.

Its warnings, on the other hand, discourage the reader from a lethargic, deficient spiritual experience. The concern here is sickness and weakness.

Simply being alive spiritually isn't enough; we must be healthy. Although saints share the same life, there are different conditions of that life. There are also different kinds of unhealthy conditions. Hebrews speaks to each.

Reading descriptions of such unhealthy conditions in this epistle brings to mind three categories. One is young Christians, who are undeveloped spiritually. Another is older Christians who have grown somewhat but who are now stunted or underdeveloped in their growth. But there are others who may have grown quite a bit and accomplished quite a lot. They are likely to be, at least religiously, alert and active. Yet their spiritual gains have become perverted, their achievements corrupted. Such can only be classified as misdeveloped.

While medical professionals don't customarily speak of infancy as an unhealthy condition, it is a precarious stage of growth since an infant needs to grow promptly, and in infancy any number of things can go wrong quickly. Such precautions as early and periodic screening are taken to insure children build immunities, gain strength, and become fully functional. Infancy is a dangerous condition of health. So, too, is spiritual infancy.

Young Christians have just been born again, babes in Christ. Sins are forgiven, but they have not yet performed righteously. Heaven is directly ahead, but many frightful things stand in the way.

What a saved sinner did by himself to render salvation actual is so little compared with what Christ did on his behalf to make it possible, he is tempted to think there remains little or nothing for him to do. Since he received life by simple faith, why can he not just relax in that same faith?

I hear certain mottos for the Christian life: "Just have faith,"—"Only believe,"—and "Keep the faith." These are more ejaculations of hope than testimonies of experience. The Bible contains certain statements that sound a little like these, but the Bible means something quite different from what the sloganeers make them sound. This is not at all the language of the Epistle to the Hebrews.

What is an infant Christian to do? Where does he go from here? Undeveloped now, he must yet develop spiritually. The freshness is sweet, but it must ripen.

Frequently, this misdevelopment is our fault—the fault of those who invited the infant believer to the altar and then left him there. We may have pursued him evangelistically, but failed to follow up.

Hebrews offers some good, workable suggestions for the care and feeding of young Christians. Better yet, it urges many excellent directions for the young Christian also. It tells exactly what to do to begin new life in Christ and to keep it growing. The young believer shouldn't be discouraged by statements of some old-time Christians who must confess to years between acceptance of Christ as Savior and surrender to him as Lord. However usual that may be, it isn't in the slightest normal.

The new believer shouldn't settle for anything less than everything God has promised as soon as he chooses to give it.

If others cheat themselves, he mustn't buy into their loss.

The most serious danger in spiritual youth is growing old without growing up. There is a natural limit to infancy, and we have no way to extend it. Growing old is not our choice; growing up is.

Hebrews is a book for young Christians. Mostly, it encourages them, but it also warns them.

If a young Christian fails to respond to the exhortations and refuses the warnings, he becomes an old, ungrown Christian. He is stunted, which is a second dangerous condition of the Christian life.

No one stays young. Many spend all their lives in a condition of stunted spiritual development. No longer can they be considered undeveloped since some growth is inevitable. They are underdeveloped. Early freshness is gone and, without ripening, they have dried up.

This group comprises a terrible percentage of the typical church, family, or other group of Christians. Many of us are among them.

We have been Christians for a long time, but we don't seem any closer to God than when we started out in the new life. In fact, we have seen better days. We had more joy and reality when we were first saved than after all these years.

The picture that comes to mind is of a soldier with hash-marks—one diagonal stripe for each three years of enlistment, from cuff to elbow. But above the elbow are placed no chevrons of rank earned, and on his chest are displayed no ribbons of decorations awarded. He is a veteran of years but not victories.

The image becomes less accurate when I recall that the army no longer tolerates such deadwood. It wisely enforces a very effective up-or-out policy. The army develops responsible leaders but gets rid of those who won't fight or produce.

Our Lord, I suppose, is more gracious and merciful than to enforce the "out." Yet he does insist upon the "up." Those who exploit the former and ignore the latter are stunted Christians.

Too bad, our Christianity isn't as visibly distinctive as an army uniform. If we had any awareness at all, we couldn't bear to pass in review with our years in ranks but no decoration for achievement or courage.

For many of us, something went wrong,—though we don't know just what. Or if we know, we have worked hard to forget it. This condition needs close watching, because those with it have seen such little spiritual fruit that we find it difficult to recognize its absence.

Some such people consider themselves to be world-weary but faithful warriors. Yet they participate in the world much more than they are willing to admit—or, even, able to recognize. Some have no idea of who the Enemy is and where he is.

There was a time when God did breathtaking things in our lives. When brothers and sisters told what he also worked in their lives, a lump came to our throats because we knew exactly what they meant.

The world seemed a beautiful place, and we thrived in it. Each day we got up and thanked God for another day in which to enjoy him. There were things to do for the Lord, and the only problem was there didn't seem to be enough time to get them all done. We enjoyed our friends and had compassion for our enemies. We enjoyed God, of course. The big surprise was that we enjoyed ourselves also.

No more. Now we highlight all the ugly things, and all things once thought beautiful we look on as fake. Each new day fades to another old day. We do some things but only to be doing something, not to get anything done. "Friends" become deceitful enemies, and enemies are the only people who can be "trusted." We respect God, of course. The bitterest disappointment is that we now hate ourselves.

I know a number of sweet, trusting elderly saints who are near death. Rightly, they long to be in the immediate presence of their lovely Lord. What a glorious hope they have! Nonetheless, even they tend to give up too soon. Any time before the moment the Lord actually calls is too soon to give up on a life he gave at such great cost and for such grand purposes.

An even larger number just think themselves too tired to go on. For them, heaven isn't an attractive goal as much as it is a cop-out from the responsibilities of life. If they were really as heavenly minded as they profess, they wouldn't hold on to this world's things so tightly.

It's reasonable to think that many sincere Christian believers fall into such a state for a while. That is, they honestly grow weary of the struggles in this life and long for the greater glory of heaven.

However, one of two things happens within a short time. They recover and go on from that momentary romance. Or they hold to, and even exaggerate, the academic doctrine of heaven and degenerate into a state of spiritual irresponsibility and indifference.

Do you, perhaps, fit in here? Apathetic about life, no feeling?

To be angry with God would give hope of an argument. Sometimes we're not angry—we just don't care anymore. We don't argue with God. We don't even talk to him much.

And there's no joy. There was a time when a soul coming to Christ brought floods of tears to our eyes. Now, those who go forward at the invitation seem such a nuisance because it means the service will run over.

For some there seems to be no sense of things being real and vital and vibrant. It is dangerous to be young for long, but we can enjoy freshness even if undeveloped. It is alarming to be stunted because we are dried and underdeveloped when we need nourishment and strength for the journey.

To nourish and strengthen is a goal of Hebrews. It is a book for stunted Christians.

Still another dangerous condition of the Christian life is perversion. If the young are fresh and the stunted dried, the perverted Christian is spoiled. He has had too much and thrown it away. He isn't ignorant, and he hasn't stopped learning—he just misuses what he knows well.

Often this Christian has sharpened his skills keenly, but he has since abused them and injured himself. Now spiritually crippled, it is not unusual for him to hurt, almost sadistically, those he professes to help.

When we were spiritually young, we needed to begin our development. If that became stunted and we stood underdeveloped, we could start there and grow more. Sometimes, however, a Christian has so hardened and so corrupted himself by tolerating sin and practicing evil, despite the opportunity for continued growth, he literally perverts the spiritual skills he once used well. The moral values that were once so enriching and ethical standards that were once so productive have become monstrously corrupted. He is misdeveloped.

No person is quite so sick as the experienced Christian who grinds spiritual food underfoot and feeds on the world's garbage. There is no person quite so dangerous as the religious person who wields religious devices to destroy spiritual opportunities.

Some, in this condition, are consciously evil and rebellious. Not all, however, are sinister; a good number are deeply earnest and act with strong convictions.

Such have really grown well, and honestly try to be "good Christians." They listen to sermons and read books on holy living. They attend—we hope—evangelistic meetings, Bible conferences, and denominational conventions.

One put it this way:

I'm gonna keep goin' to the meetin's 'til the Spirit hits me. Then I'll have it, and I ain't never gonna lose it.

Another, much more sober, said:

This old world just doesn't have any attractions left for me. It's an evil world, and these are "the last days." There is just nothing we can do to change things. The Bible warns us. We've got to expect trials and tribulations. We're going to be persecuted for the name of Christ. Any moment now Jesus is coming again and we'll be caught up to meet him in the air. Then he'll save us from the Great Tribulation, which those remaining on earth will suffer. Then we'll return with him to set up his Kingdom. Then we'll all be kings and reign with him. But until then, all we can do is "watch and wait."

Here is the expectation of still another of these quite sincere people:

This world is not my home; I'm just passing through. I'm a citizen of heaven, and my home is beyond the skies. I just can't wait until the Lord calls me home. But I'll be faithful until he calls.

I feel uneasy as I quote these people, who actually did make these statements. I don't want anyone to think I am cartooning him, or someone might think I'm poking fun. These are embarrassingly close to statements most of us have made at some time.

Sometimes the people quoted were just being ridiculous, and they should be called down for their foolishness. Few of us would go so far as they, even though we might agree with them.

More often, I feel, these people were honest and sincere. These are accurate statements of their faith. Faith, they are convinced, is a gift from God and all the Christian can do is to keep it gratefully until the day of the Lord when such faith will be rewarded. Faith is from a gracious God, and Almighty God will do all there is to do in his way and in his time.

When I was an undergraduate, something over thirty years ago, there was a slogan: "Let go, and let God."

I value that advice, and wish to practice it. Yet it is an incomplete statement. It doesn't tell me what it is I should let go of or what it is I should let God do. Surely, not everything because that would be nonsense. Yet that is the naive assumption more than a few earnest Christian believers make.

The third condition of some Christians, then, is to be aware of spiritual values and quite likely to be religiously involved. But faith for them is passive and a possession. Not so for the New Testament writers, and Hebrews is most explicit on the matter. So Hebrews is also for the Christian whose spiritual experience has become perverted.

At least these three conditions of the Christian life are dangerous. The young Christian is fresh but *undeveloped*. The stunted Christian is dried and *underdeveloped*. The perverted Christian is spoiled and *misdeveloped*.

The first is simply an infant. The second is retarded. But the last is disturbed.

THE EARLIER HEBREWS

What was the spiritual condition of the people to whom the Epistle to the Hebrews was initially written? From what the author of the epistle said to them, we can know something about them and their condition.

The first century Christians were converted by those who had known Jesus during his earthly ministry (2:3ff.), so they were second-generation believers. If their conversion were not from Judaism, they at least acquired a strong respect for the ancient Hebrew institutions and God's promises to Israel. They cherished, then, a solid theological background.

Early in their Christian lives they had endured some kind of persecution (10:32ff.), although not as severe as that which was soon to come (12:4). That earlier crisis created in them a practical expression of their faith by ministering to their brothers, especially those most affected by the persecution (6:10; 10:34). Despite these early experiences, they were by the time of the epistle no longer growing (5:11–6:20) and, indeed, were beginning to go back (2:1ff.).

It was not that they were consciously rebelling against the gospel faith or purposely turning to something else. Rather, they were taking their faith for granted and presuming upon God's grace in the sacrifice of his Son (10:26-31). They were lethargic and sluggish in regard to their faith (3:7–4:13). In belief they were orthodox, but in practice they were heretics.

They seem to have exaggerated the effectiveness of the law. On the other hand, they depreciated the ultimacy of Christ's sacrifice (9:11–10:31) and his perfection (4:14–5:10; 7:1–8:13). They also took lightly the promise of heaven made to them (11:13-16).

They were staunchly traditional about religious requirements, but were thoughtless and careless about spiritual opportunities.

These people, whoever they were, possessed salvation yet were neglecting to live it. They were in danger not only of failing to reach the fullness of their salvation but, in some sense, of losing their present experience of salvation. Instead of gaining the better things promised, they risked losing the good things already received and being left with only the lesser things of the past.

"Hebrews" is a curious name for a letter, once you think about it. One would expect the word "Jews." During the exile in Babylon (600-536 B.C.), the people of Israel began to be called "Jews," those of the tribe of Judah.

In the New Testament, they were almost always called Jews,

but not Hebrews. This was an ethnic term, used before the exile and especially before the nation Israel entered into the land of promise.

It was the term used during the wilderness wanderings narrated in the Book of Numbers. These people had exited from bondage in Egypt, yet refused to enter into God's promise. They were, in Numbers' story, wandering aimlessly and pointlessly in the Sinai desert. They were, in fact, dying in that wilderness without ever entering into the land. That is probably why these first century Christians were called "Hebrews."

The readers may also have been racially Jews, but that is not at all the point. They were, regardless of race or religious background, immature Christians. This is the point of the epistle.

Like those ancient Hebrews, these Christians had received an exodus from sin's bondage and had been promised a destiny. Also like the literal Hebrews, these figurative "Hebrews" rebelled, refusing to enter into what God had promised. They, too, were wandering aimlessly in the arid wilderness of spiritual immaturity.

These "Hebrews" were in danger of falling in that wilderness and never entering into all that God had promised. Those Hebrews actually did die in the wilderness and never entered into the land. God wouldn't let them.

Before we came to this epistle, then, there were two generations of Hebrews. Those of Moses' day were Hebrews ethnically. This is the literal reference. They had experienced these things physically, and it was acted out geographically.

There were also those mentioned by the writer of Hebrews who may also have been ethnically Hebrew (more specifically, Jewish). At least, they were "Hebrews" spiritually and morally. The figurative use of "Hebrew" is the significant meaning for them.

For years there have been questions about the authorship of this letter. There isn't much to say about it because the author says nothing.

He doesn't attach his name to the letter, and he doesn't say anything about himself within it. This was no accident. The first readers knew fully well who wrote, and a name wasn't necessary. More important, the author didn't want the readers to think about him. He did not forget to sign his letter nor assume it to be unnecessary. In fact, he seems to have considered self-reference inappropriate as it would have been counter-productive to his purpose.

Part of the religious "big deal" these Hebrews were making for themselves was their relationship to the writer. They seem to have followed him as a religious figurehead rather than emulating his example as a spiritual leader.

Enough of this nonsense, the writer was saying. They must be followers of Christ, not of any human. So far as Christ's appointed undershepherds, the readers had their local church leaders and human-level loyalty must be given to them.

> Obey your leaders and submit to their authority. They keep watch over you as men who must give an account. Obey them so that their work will be a joy, not a burden, for that would be of no advantage to you (Heb. 13:17).

What, then, should be their attitude toward the writer?

> Pray for us. We are sure that we have a clear conscience and desire to live honorably in every way. I particularly urge you to pray so that I may be restored to you soon. (vv. 18, 19).

Not only is authorship unimportant in understanding the message; to forget the matter seems almost a help. If we are not literally to forget the question, surely we must not let any dispute about it keep us from understanding the message and responding to its appeal.

I have met a few people who felt that Paul was the author. They were more interested in profitless speculations as to whom the author might be than they were in being obedient to what he wrote. Most were college sophomores.

I have met others who thought it heresy to say anyone but Paul was the author and spent all their time in defensive argument.

Nothing would have displeased the writer of Hebrews more than either of those attitudes. For such reasons, we are not going to pursue it further. It doesn't matter who wrote the Epistle to the Hebrews. What does matter is knowing who the "Hebrews" are.

WE "HEBREWS"

Yes, we are "Hebrews," for there were three generations of them:

(1) those of the nation Israel in Moses' day, wandering in the Sinai wilderness.

(2) those Jews (of whatever mixture) of some Greek city in apostolic days, wandering in a spiritual wilderness.

(3) those of American communities in our day, also wandering, in our own spiritual wilderness.

We have all gone through our miraculous exodus from the death of sin. We are born again and saved from that past sin. We are truly and forever members of the family of God. We are the People. We have been offered the promise.

But not all promptly took the promise and stayed with it. To do so would be the normal procedure, but it doesn't seem to be the usual. My own experience is the more typical. I didn't take the promise. I turned back from the promise and, for an inexcusable length of time, wandered aimlessly in the wilderness of faithless rebellion.

As we consider the description of the first readers of this epistle, they seem familiar. Most of us could translate a few of the terms to our own settings and the rest would fit.

We don't, of course, make too much of the Law of Moses. However, we often make too much of the rules of our churches. While we don't have a Day of Atonement, we do have things like the annual revival meetings.

We take salvation for granted and drift away from its reality. This causes our hearts to become insensitive to the better things belonging to our salvation. We fall in serious danger of never entering the best thing—God's promised rest.

The purpose of the Epistle to the Hebrews, then, is to exhort us to become active in our present experience with God's salvation. That alone will enable us to possess the land of all that God has promised. Yet we must do this while it is still "today."

Could any of us, like those Hebrews, drop dead right there?

Could it be that we might have received eternal salvation only to lose the opportunity of experiencing all of it? That is what this epistle is all about.

The five warnings do not advise us that such might happen if we have bad luck. They assure us that this will happen unless we accept good fortune.

On the other hand, the five exhortations challenge us on to the specific things that qualify us to enter into all that has been promised.

ETERNAL SECURITY OR LOSS OF SALVATION?

Are you going to tell me—I can hear some Calvinist worrying— that a Christian can lose his salvation? You're going to tell them—I can hear some Arminian hoping—that a Christian can lose his salvation!

Wrong both times.

Such oversimplified dogmas are both partly correct and partly incorrect. You might have expected as much. Genuine Christians equally earnest about the Christian life and serious about Bible study just could not develop such constructive ministries if both did not have hold of at least some substantial element of the biblical doctrine.

By the same token, genuine Christians equally earnest about the Christian life and serious about Bible study just could not come to such opposite positions if both did not miss at least some substantial element of the biblical doctrine.

Did the writer of this epistle believe in the doctrine of eternal security? Of course he did. Did his readers? You bet they did, and this was at the heart of their problem. They not only believed it—they exploited it. They presumed outrageously upon it. It was to defeat this shameless exploitation and to overcome its terrible presumption that this epistle had to be written.

Salvation is eternally secure. The New Testament teaches so throughout. The writer to the Hebrews believed it. Nonetheless, he doesn't talk about it. In fact, if you read this epistle closely and in isolation from the rest of Scripture, you can very easily become convinced that the writer did not believe in eternal security and that, moreover, he taught one can lose the salvation God gave as a gift of grace.

However, he didn't write this epistle to convince of eternal security. He wrote to convince of another serious aspect of our salvation and to persuade us to lay hold of it.

No writer of Scripture argued the doctrine of eternal security. The Bible does not even argue the existence of God. Yet why should the Eternal God, who made man and confronts him and judges him, try to prove to the creature that his Creator exists? So, too, God does not argue that the salvation he gives is eternally secure. He just gives it and keeps it. God's promise is that he gives us eternal life. This is what he said, and this is what he does.

If a person can explain how one can lose anything that is *eternal*, then we can begin to listen to arguments for the loss of eternal life. We can't construct a four-sided triangle since a triangle, by definition, has but three sides. Add a fourth side, and it is no longer a triangle. If eternal life can be lost, the language has no meaning.

The best possible and the final argument for eternal security is that God said he gives eternal life (John 3:16). The fact is as certain as this, and the proof as simple.

FALLING BACK

When you read such expressions as "press on" and "don't fall back," you may envision images of running. They come naturally from the author who challenges; "Let us run with perseverance the race marked out for us" (12:1).

One cannot avoid the use of the imagery of running when talking about either this epistle or life itself. I understood more clearly what the author means as I began distance running. As this developed into competitive running, I understood still better what had been written.

There are many analogies in running, specifically distance running, to living life as the active practice of faith. After all, life is lived as a race is run.

You can understand that one of the greatest temptations in running is to walk. But there is more. To walk when I am committed to run is to take the first step to dropping out.

I construct logical sounding excuses for a little walking. But they fly in the face of experience. Telling myself, "A little walking won't hurt," is a betrayal of the fact that I have already decided to drop out. The decision is in the subconscious at the moment, but it has been made. The fact is, walking is a contradiction to running. It is destructive of the run. I am referring, of course, to surrender to a walk when I could be and should be running. Such is the violation of a commitment.

I have learned several things in daily runs: The *sooner* I walk, the more *frequently* I will walk. The *more frequently* I walk, the *longer* I will walk. The *longer* I walk, the *less of a run* it is. Eventually, it no longer is a *run* at all.

The most significant negative lesson I learned in my first marathon was not to fall back. Once someone starts walking in a marathon, he begins to think of himself as a walker and not a runner. One can't expect too much from a walker.

A walker also becomes a loner or, worse still, a member of bad company. In a small race, when one falls back, there are no runners around from whom to take encouragement. No one sets a positive example. There is no one to yell, "Come on, guy, you can do it!"

In larger races there are always walkers to offer nonembarrassing and nondemanding company. You put from mind the thousands who are ahead, some having already finished, and consider only the stragglers. You exchange excuses with other failures so that "success" takes on a new, strange definition. (It's amazing how agreeable such people can be when in each other's company.)

You think of an unending number of reasons you're not running. With every fabrication, it is easier to keep walking. The final excuse comes, "Well, it was only a marathon. There are plenty of those. It just wasn't my day. Maybe next time. Why worry about it? I did better than those still in bed."

Such a thought is self-defeating. With this attitude you may just not enter again. If you do, the likelihood of your finishing or finishing well is reduced in direct proportion to the number of times you pull this on yourself.

Every marathon has duffers who, for all practical purposes, dropped out around the fifteen-mile marker. They have walked (perhaps strolled) from there and, in a geographical sense, cross the finish line. But the clock has been stopped, the chute flags have been taken up, and the crowd is watching the runners being presented with earned awards.

For them there is satisfaction and celebration. For the walkers, it is shame and pretense.

As they tell the story, "I *entered* the marathon" or "I was *in* it." When they say they "finished," they strain language, if not also truth. Surely, they cannot say they *accomplished* the race. I'm not so sure it is fair even to say they "did a marathon."

The eternal, spiritual life with which God has gifted believers is not a thing to be finished religiously. It is an experience to be accomplished spiritually.

We dare not be pseudo-Calvinists, who think accepting Christ is all there is to salvation. With final salvation eternally secure, such people refuse the ongoing experience of salvation.

And we dare not be pseudo-Arminians, who think the race is over because they have reached "sinless perfection." With much salvation already experienced, they refuse to run the race that is still set before them.

Make no mistake about it. Religious walking is not the spiritual run. We are not "out for a stroll," because our Lord calls upon us to perform in a race. Life is lived as a race is run—with persistence. The first step to dropping out of spiritual experience is to walk "just a little bit" when it is running that is required.

Our author warns us: Don't fall back! Don't slow down your spiritual growth. Don't let up the effort. Don't tolerate discouragement. Don't kid yourself.

The reason is, you'll drop out. That's how it starts, and this is how it ends.

THE ENCOURAGEMENTS AND WARNINGS
The writer of Hebrews gave five exhortations and five warnings:

Lay hold	2:1-4
Do it	3:7–4:13
Go on	5:11–6:20
Draw near	10:19-30
Build up	12:12-17

The word *exhortation* is a technical term of rhetoric which indentifies an encouraging challenge. In terms of grammar, it uses the subjunctive mood and is in the first person plural, "us." It is typically translated "let us." In this epistle we find exhortations, or challenges, expressed like this:

> "Let us, therefore strive to enter that rest" (4:11, RSV).
> "Therefore let us leave the elementary doctrine of Christ and go on" (6:1, RSV).
> "Let us draw near with a true heart in full assurance of faith" (10:22, RSV).
> "Let us hold fast the confession of our hope without wavering" (10:23, RSV).
> "Let us consider how to stir up one another to love and good works" (10:24, RSV).

Perhaps the term "exhortation" seems a little too technical. Then think of it as "encouragement," an earnest encouragement strongly issued. It is not, "Let's see if we can do a little better." It is, "Let's get moving!"

The writer also gave five warnings:

> Don't drift away (2:1-4).
> Don't disbelieve (3:7-19).
> Don't fall away (4:1-13).
> Don't walk away (6:1-8).
> Don't fall apart (10:26-31).

While an exhortation is positive and constructive, a warning is negative and prohibitive. An exhortation encourages us to do something good and promises desirable results if we comply. A warning cautions against doing something bad and assures us of undesirable consequences if we resist the warning.

Most of us need both encouragement and discouragement, challenges and warnings. And we need both in regard to the same concerns. We benefit when someone comes at us from both sides, showing the positive and the negative.

It should be no surprise, then, that this deeply concerned writer does just this. The texts for the warnings are the same as for the exhortations. The writer presents them together and balanced. He puts the emphasis upon the exhortations and considers the whole epistle "a word of exhortation" (13:22) concerning God's salvation.

Yet he gives full treatment, even if secondary, to the warnings. They dare not be neglected because they are crucial to his argument. They contribute the contrast that is essential for balanced perspective.

It is the warnings, I fear, that most people remember who haven't studied Hebrews carefully. These warnings are, in fact, one of the principal causes for people not even wanting to read the epistle. Those who isolate the warnings out of context and exaggerate them out of proportion lose doctrinal perspective completely and come up with the most grotesque teachings possible.

Others "solve" the problem wrongly by claiming the rest of the epistle for Christians like themselves but write off all the warnings—yet only the warnings—as applying exclusively to the unsaved.

I understand their motives, and I respect their goals. However, the doctrine of eternal security does not need our discounting these five warnings from Scripture or reassigning them from the writer's Spirit-directed targets. If we did, we would destroy one of the Bible's most crucial doctrines of salvation. Here only—and in the Epistle of James—is this aspect of salvation treated.

The Epistle of James suffers the same fate as these passages in Hebrews from nervous dabblers in the Bible. James and Hebrews stand in marked contrast to Paul's epistles to the Galatians and then to the Romans. They are actually significant progressions beyond the doctrine of the possession of salvation and move to the opportunity for experiencing salvation.

Galatians and Romans say, "Here is how you get salvation." James and Hebrews say, "Here is how you use salvation."

Hebrews, in turn, differs from James and is peculiar to itself. This is nowhere more evident than in its unique exhortations and warnings.

One of the reasons some people exaggerate the warnings out of proportion is that they are genuinely terrible. One gasps for breath at the audacity of the writer. One can hardly believe these warnings to be the Word of a loving God. Could this be a forgiving Father talking to his weak children?

The warnings should scare the socks off us. At the same time, we should let them also drive us to the encouragement of the exhortations. If we respond to the exhortations, they will lift us right out of our shoes.

Long-standing but failing Christians are exhorted to persistent growth and warned about the spiritually fatal consequences of their indifference.

The theme of Hebrews can be put simply: Let's live actively, determined to accomplish life.

TWO

LAY HOLD, LEST YOU DRIFT AWAY

HEBREWS 2:1-4

Society has spawned still another critical age, retirement. No longer a few years of ease shortly before death, retirement is becoming a protracted period of idleness after an unsatisfying occupation. For some it seems death will never arrive to break the boredom.

No longer making million dollar sales over lunch, a man now consumes all afternoon and half a tank of gas to save 98¢ in a sale on floor wax. For an old farmer, painting the garage door is as large a project as was getting the crop in. Labor contracts between hostile sides were negotiated calmly by the man who now sulks out of the house because his wife wants him to move a chair again.

People who refused to work at church because of "employment conflicts" now won't because they have "a right to our freedom." They don't go to Sunday school since children make them nervous, and the evening services run too late. Little things bother, but nothing is big enough to interest.

They never chose this mood, and they never noticed it coming. It all came about by degrees as they gradually let go of good things from youth. They've just aged and wearied. They wore themselves out doing nothing. While they feel they may as well give up, they mope along by habit.

Yet, such people did choose. They abdicated from being positive decision makers by deciding to make none. They did not lay hold of life and are now drifting from full life.

To use the word retirement, an economic term, is to suggest social and emotional conditions, but it is at least as much spiritual. And spiritual life itself follows a similar pattern.

Spiritual growth can come quickly, yet seldom does it come suddenly. Those spectacular bursts of religious zeal are likely to be nothing more than just that and to disappear as suddenly, with as little cause.

Genuine spiritual growth is usually not recognized by the one growing until the person reaches a milestone. Looking back over the distance recently covered, one realizes he has been living spiritually with a strength he hadn't enjoyed previously.

It is the more likely to be recognized by a brother or sister who hadn't been watching every moment and can compare distant points more sharply. The more mature the other person is, the more clearly will the growth be seen.

So, too, is spiritual deterioration. When we weaken and become foolish, we are deteriorating rather than growing. Although outright and dramatic rebellion does occur, it is not usual. Like growth, it is more likely to be gradual and unnoticed for a long while until something draws it to attention.

Drawing spiritual drifting to our attention is precisely what the writer did in Hebrews 2:1-4, as he exhorted us to lay hold so we don't drift.

This text presents, together, the first exhortation and the first warning.

"We must," the writer said, "pay more careful attention . . . to what we have heard." This is the exhortation, or strong encouragement.

The same sentence begins the warning:"—Lest we drift away from it" (RSV). He reasoned with his readers: "—How shall we escape if we ignore ["neglect," KJV] such a great salvation?"

The first encouragement, then, is to lay hold of the teaching about salvation that we have heard. The first warning is the fact that we ourselves could be in danger of drifting away from this teaching and the inescapable consequence of neglecting to use our salvation.

We must deliberately lay hold of salvation in order to avoid losing our grip on the life of salvation. If we rise to the challenge and lay hold of salvation in the fullest sense, we will experience the power of a saving life.

AN EXHORTATION TO LAY HOLD   Hebrews 2:1

In the first chapter of Hebrews, the writer acknowledged the adequate character of salvation as mediated through the Law of Moses and the messages delivered by angels. He was thrilled to describe the superiority of salvation directly through God's Son, Jesus Christ. More than superior, salvation through Christ is ultimate and final. It is *The Great Salvation.*

"Therefore" begins the second chapter. Because of the greatness of salvation in God's Son, "We must pay more careful attention . . . to what we have heard."

The King James Version translation, "give the more earnest heed," might well put it even more strongly to the minds of some. Although the standard definitions are rather the same, "heed" does connote to some the expectation of response. It does when a person says, "Heed my word."

If "attention," the word used in most versions, doesn't seem strong enough to us for the idea, it is likely that we haven't paid much attention to anything. To these things we must.

In the original language of the writer, this verb is one of two nautical terms used to create an analogy. It is the word Greeks used for the task of tying a boat to a dock. It means, literally, "to moor a ship."

When I was in boot camp at Great Lakes, Illinois, I learned a new official vocabulary. In addition to *deck* for "floor" and *hatch* for "door," I learned a sailor never says "I tied the boat." He says "I secured the craft."

In this case, there is good reason to use the word "secure" in place of "tie." I learned new knots for *lines* (not "ropes") that have specific purposes. When a seaman brings a craft in to the dock, he secures it. And it stays secure. He makes sure because it is his job.

I wish I had understood these things and had the skills when I was a waterfront director at a Wisconsin Bible camp. At the end of one boating period, I neatly tied all the rowboats to the dock. Before I left the waterfront, I checked to see that each boat was tied in its place so that I could leave without worry and forget all about them.

As I went to the dining hall a while later, I glanced down the hill to the lake. Although I thought the boats were farther from the dock than I had intended, I assumed I had left more play in the rope than I realized. It didn't look as neat as I would have liked, but it wasn't worth the trouble to retie them or to be late for supper.

After supper, I stood on the hill talking with good friends. I sensed the boats were still farther from the dock. I really knew I hadn't tied them as closely as I should have. I would do so hereafter. They now seemed a little farther away from the dock than before, but it was still nothing to worry about. If I remembered it, I could always pull them in and retie them before bedtime.

Later, I realized the boats were drifting. I was so preoccupied, however, I didn't respond to what I actually knew.

During the evening service, the wind picked up and I thought about the boats. I really didn't feel like going all the way to the waterfront. I went only because I had little interest in the sermon.

As I went down the hill, I realized the boats were no longer tied to the dock. They weren't even near the dock, but were far from shore, drifting farther still toward the middle of the lake.

I had watched this happen throughout the process. I hadn't secured the boats, and they drifted slowly away. They had gone some distance before I recognized anything at all. When I became aware something was happening, I assumed it to be of no significance. I put off action thinking there was plenty of time to do something and that my something would be good enough. It was only after a wind arose and the boats were already beyond reach from shore that they moved quickly.

If a full storm had hit suddenly and the waves quickly washed the boats away, I, and everyone else, would have arisen to the emergency. We are great in crises. I would have mobilized the camp, and I would have been the hero of the hour. But I did not secure the boats to the fixed mooring so they drifted away without my notice.

Few of us rebel and storm out of God's house. We just lose interest and fade away. Not very often does the Enemy come in like a flood. When he does, we mobilize and drive him back. That's exactly why he doesn't often come in like a flood. It is much more successful to encourage spiritual drifting. It takes him a little longer, but the end result is the same. And the results are long-lasting.

The great danger in the Christian life is not open rebellion.

It is quiet drifting. Therefore, the great requirement for Christian living is to lay hold of what we have heard. We must secure ourselves to the doctrines of spiritual living, lest we drift away from the life of the Spirit.

The message we have heard is of salvation from sin through dependence upon the finished work of Christ. We were literally dead in sin, and we are now literally alive in Christ. Our earthly life has been changed into eternal life. What we have heard is that Christ made a difference in us when he became our Savior and we are, under his lordship, to live that difference.

As the author applied the exhortations and warnings to the practice of faith he lists specific acts by which we "lay hold" and "hold unswervingly to the hope we profess" (10:23.) These demonstrate two grasps of the basic commitment, the foundation of faith. We grasp them firmly without ever loosening the grip. Still holding them firmly, we reach beyond to yet greater things built upon them.

Laying hold of what we have heard is not a manner of speaking or a mystical state. It is specific acts of laying hold, as shown in the language of Chapters 12 and 13:

> Let us throw off everything that hinders and the sin that so easily entangles, and let us run with perseverance the race marked out for us (12:1). . . . Endure hardship as discipline (12:7). . . . See to it that no one misses the grace of God and that no bitter root grows up to cause trouble (12:15). . . . Do not forget to entertain strangers (13:2). . . . Marriage should be honored by all (13:4). . . . Remember your leaders, who spoke the word of God to you. Consider the outcome of their way of life and imitate their faith (13:7). . . . Do not be carried away by all kinds of strange teachings (13:9). . . . Do not forget to do good and to share with others (13:16). . . . Obey your leaders and submit to their authority (13:17).

These are basic acts of early Christian living. Although possible for spiritual infants, they remain essential for growth and life at every stage of the Christian life. Childlike acts are different from childish acts.

Eating meals is childlike. Childishness is refusing for silly reasons to eat nourishing food. Some, in their childish way, neglect the spiritual nourishment of corporate worship and the preaching of God's Word. The author found it necessary to warn against "neglecting to meet together as is the habit of some" (10:25).

Some are in the habit of saying, "I've been a Christian for a long time, and missing one more church service isn't going to hurt me. You don't get a blessing by just sitting in a pew, you know."

Quite true. But the chances are greater than sitting in an easy chair at home. Going to church is no guarantee, but it is one thing we can do to get things back on course. Going to church is no guarantee, but neglecting to do so is a good way to insure not getting back on track.

More than a few Christians dismiss the value of regular worship as being old stuff because they were forced to do it as a child. That thinking goes in the wrong direction. Better to say, "If I could attend as a child, I can lead as an adult."

There were times when I said, "I really don't know if I'll get anything out of church today or not." Some of those times I stayed home and never did know. Other times I went and found out. Usually I did get something. Sometimes, to be frank, there wasn't much there. Even then, I got something just by doing the right thing.

No matter how often we have attended worship or how much we have already gained from it, worship is one of the things to lay hold of. And when we don't recognize why we must go, it is likely to be the time when we most need to go. Something has slipped, and we'd better get back to basics.

I once went to an Alcoholics Anonymous meeting in New York City. I attended a beginners meeting under assignment in my doctoral work. The first three to tell their stories were not beginners but forgetful veterans returned for beginner's lessons. All realized they had violated that day three basic rules of staying dry: never get lonely, hungry, or tired. While none had taken a drink, each realized he or she had no right to feel safe. If they had neglected the basic rules, they felt they needed to go back to a beginner's session where those are established.

It wouldn't hurt to go through confirmation classes or church membership sessions once every few years. Evangelistic services, in addition to the principal goal of conversions, can serve well as reminders of these basic things we have heard.

Many spiritual acts have a quantity about them that we can measure in ourselves. Can I identify the last time I prayed or read Scripture and recall how much time I spent? Add up the total offerings thus far this year. Put marks on the calendar each Sunday you attend worship.

Good scores on such exercises do not prove we have arrived. But bad scores betray we haven't begun, or that we must go back and lay hold again.

Don't minimize the value of those things we have heard. Lay hold of them lest you drift from them. We have heard about salvation, but we haven't always heard enough. Or we don't understand what we have heard. The answer comes quickly that we are saved from sin. But we are not so quick to answer the question, "For what are we saved?"

No one has had the nerve to say it, but I suspect some think it is enough for Christ to have saved us from past sin. From now on, we are on our own. Would anyone dare say we don't need salvation from the sins yet to be committed? Why, then, do we hear salvation spoken of only in the past tense and so seldomly in the present and future tenses?

We are not on our own, and we are saved for living the life given. Not only did Christ come to give life, but to give it more abundantly (John 10:10). Abundant life becomes ours by growth, not by replacement. We don't abandon new birth in order to go on to maturity. Nor can we learn more by neglecting what we have heard. We lay hold of what we have heard and reach beyond for the rest. Not only have we been saved from past sins, but we are to be saved from future sin. Not only are we to be saved from the guilt of having committed additional sin, we are to be saved from the temptation to commit it.

Salvation doesn't just close the door to sin's old bondage. It also opens new opportunities for righteousness. The goal of salvation is not as much a rescue from sin as it is deliverance to holiness.

Many drifting Christians have been paying strong attention to the first aspect of salvation, reception of new life and its eternal security. Nevertheless, it hasn't kept them from drifting from their present experience with salvation. They were *theologically* secured to regeneration. But they were not *doctrinally* secured to sanctification.

By the term *theology,* I mean an abstract concept of what a thing is ideally. *Doctrine* is a concrete principle by which an ideal thing becomes actual.

Regeneration describes our being brought from the death of sin to the life of the Spirit. Sanctification describes being set apart from sin and evil. We must believe theology, and practice doctrine. We must start with regeneration, and go on to sanctification.

It is the difference between being born and growing up, between being a baby and an adult. We begin as babies but go on to become adults.

There is a difference between a thing *happening to* me and *my experiencing* a thing. A person observes a happening; one participates in an experience.

As I was driving to work, an accident *happened* to another car. I saw it. As I was driving home, I *experienced* an accident with my car. I felt it.

Salvation is more than a happening or a possession. It is an experience. And it must be continually and forever exerienced.

Being an experienced Minnesotan, I own several pairs of gloves and mittens. When I go out and the wind-chill is $-40°$, I do not tuck my mittens away in a pocket so I won't lose them. I put them on my hands and use them. I do not own mittens in case I should need them. I experience them because I need them now.

It is a glorious thing for anyone to possess salvation. It is a gift of God's grace. It is an eternal possession. Because of it, the one who has it will enter heaven and live eternally with the Lord.

However, we must lay hold of salvation so that we use it. Every time we commit a sin, we must confess that sin and be saved from it. I am always in need of more of that salvation— salvation from sin.

Every time sin appears on the scene, I must ask the Holy Spirit to empower me so that I am saved from committing that sin. This, too, is salvation. It is part of my salvation, and my salvation is not complete without it. There is more to our salvation than what we now have. Let's get all of it and keep getting it. Secure yourself to the opportunities salvation opens so you cannot drift from the experience of salvation.

A WARNING NOT TO NEGLECT *Hebrews 2:2, 3a*

Having exhorted to lay hold, the writer of Hebrews warns about the consequences of neglecting salvation.

He asks, "How shall we escape if we ignore such a great salvation?"

Nervous people anxiously ask, "Escape what?" Minds jump quickly to the things from which one might want to escape. Evangelists traditionally shock the unsaved by asking, "Do you want to escape hell?" So, when the words *escape* and *salvation* come in the same statement, it seems natural to connect the escape with eternal death in hell.

If so, this must refer to the unsaved. It is saying, some suggest, that an unsaved person who continues to ignore or neglect the offer of salvation cannot expect to escape hell. While that is certainly true, it is not what the Bible is saying at this point.

First, to look at just a fragment of one statement ignores its context. One statement within a book must, by its very nature, be addressed to the book's readers. The integrity of this epistle requires its having been written to Christian believers. Not only can there be no other sense to the content, this is how the early Church took it.

Second, such a conclusion ignores the first part of the sentence in which it is found. Referring back to those under the Law of Moses, people of the old covenant, it mentions the punishment, not destruction, of children's disobedience. God sent his angel-messengers to believers and not to those of the world.

Third, such a conclusion looks outside the statement for a connection when its connection is obvious within itself. How shall we escape if we neglect *what* of "such a great salvation?" The consequences of neglecting, of course! The text doesn't need to state immediately what those consequences are—the whole epistle does so!

Fourth, the word *neglect,* or "ignore," regularly refers to failure to utilize a thing already possessed. The unsaved do not neglect salvation. They reject it, even if by neglecting the offer.

The Apostle Paul warned Timothy, "Do not *neglect* your gift" (1 Tim. 4:14). You have the gift, Timothy; now use it.

The writer of Hebrews said elsewhere, "because they continued not in my covenant, and I regarded them not" (8:9, KJV). The Revised Standard Version reads: "I paid no heed to them." The same word appears in 4:14 and 8:9. If we neglect to use our salvation, it will not save us from any sin to which we failed to apply it.

As a public health nurse, my wife is responsible for many elderly and forgetful people in our community. I regularly hear her talking with patients from our home telephone, at all hours. It's almost a litany to end such conversations, "And don't forget to take your medication." A variation is, "Don't neglect your medicine."

It amuses our three children that their mother can rag on old people as well as kids. This, we know, is because she truly cares about all of us. You need to care deeply about people to keep warning and exhorting them.

One of our patients, when I was on the clinical pastoral care staff of a medical center, was a lady I first met in the emergency room in the middle of the night. They expected her to die before they could get her to surgery. They got her there, and one of the surgeons performed a piece of surgery and quite literally saved her life. Following surgery, her physician prescribed medication for her. His wisdom determined the medicine needed, and a pharmacist's skill prepared it. All she had to do was to take it. But only she could take it.

I happened to be with her when the physician explained and gave explicit directions for taking it. He told her how much to take and when. "Whenever you get sick," he advised her, "take this." He added, quite sternly, I thought, "and follow the directions."

I have spent time with grateful patients before and since then, but none praised the surgeon more than she. He walked on water, as far as she was concerned. No greater miracle had ever been performed. It was all she could think about and all she ever talked about.

When she had recovered from the surgery, a new nurse was clearing her from the ward. Each time the nurse tried to fill her in on another point of home care, the overly grateful woman would say something like, "Did I ever tell you . . . ?"

During the next couple of years, our ever-praising, loudly talkative patient was readmitted frequently. Each time it was for the same reason—she hadn't taken her medicine.

At the first readmission, she said to the admissions clerk, "The last time I was here . . ." Each time thereafter it was, "The first time I was here . . ." But she never brought her medicine with her. When asked about it—she would reassure, "Oh, I haven't lost it. It's at home—right on the top shelf of my medicine cabinet. It's almost full."

Everytime I visited her, she expected me to listen to her war story all over again. She drove her neighbors up the wall with it. But no one could get her to listen to anything about her medicine, much less take it. As long as she was in the hospital, someone could force it on her. But as soon as she returned home, it was no more medicine.

One day the head nurse spoke to me privately, with more desperation than humor, "Chaplain, would you please tell that woman to shut her mouth and take her medicine! There's nothing wrong with her that the medicine won't cure. But she's making surgery a way of life, and it's going to kill her." We agreed the funeral director could make a fortune selling her unused medicine.

Do certain people come to mind in light of this case? But the problems aren't necessarily medical. More than a few are like this about salvation. Christ saved our lives and it was, indeed, a miracle. We tell everyone about it and never stop. After a while, however, it begins to sound less like praise to God than bragging about oneself. It is almost as if Christ never saved anyone other than that person, and he did so as some special favor.

But that person doesn't keep up with the Word of God. His Bible is still on the top shelf of the bookcase where he put it after the evangelistic meetings. He keeps getting spiritually sick because he never draws nourishment from it. He keeps getting weak because he gains no strength from it. He stands during every testimony time and retells the same old story. There still is nothing wrong with the content of the story, but its telling isn't convincing as it once was. There is never a sequel. Not only does he never lead anyone to Christ, he doesn't speak of any further salvation for himself. Surely, some sin presented itself recently. If he had sought salvation from it, certainly God would have given salvation. Then there could be a new story and a new joy. But never.

More salvation, from the same sin repeated once again, might be the same song. But it would at least be another stanza. This person keeps singing the same stanza. And the tune gets flatter every time.

Our indifferent hospital patient was admitted for a final time while I was still on staff. They didn't try to take her to surgery because there was no surgical procedure remaining for her fatal condition. She just died. It was too late, not only for the long-term medicine but even for quick-fix surgery.

When this condition is true of a person spiritually, the epistle's warning must be taken seriously. Be grateful for the new birth, and never stop praising God for it. But keep well and growing by following directions. There is more to your salvation. Take it.

There is another way to recognize the tragedy of neglecting such a great salvation. It is a little like using the commercial principle of you-get-what-you-pay-for, which works reasonably well as a rule of thumb in assessing the value of a product.

A good product is good partly because costly material and skilled labor were used in it, which is finally reflected in the price. I had once talked a salesman down on a piece of office machinery. When he went to the owner for approval of a reduced price, the owner explained to me, "I can't let it go for less than the asking price. I have too much *in it*."

What God has in the salvation he offers to mankind is nothing less than the life of his Son. It is the most costly thing ever offered and carries the highest price in history. This is why the producer-owner had to pay the price himself.

When such an offer is made, we just can't afford to turn our backs on it. Most who are reading this have probably accepted salvation. But many, if not most, of us at one time or another, have gone on to neglect what we once accepted. God's decision to offer salvation as a gift would almost seem to have been self-defeating when redeemed sinners neglect the gift because it didn't cost them anything. It is such realities that cause some merchandisers to raise the price just to get potential customers to take the product more seriously. Not only is salvation at the greatest cost and highest possible price so that such would be impossible, there is a better way to create seriousness in salvation consumers. The Holy Spirit showed this to our writer, exhorting us to use and warning of non-use.

There is still another principle that can help us understand the consequences of neglecting the use of salvation. We know that the greater potential a thing has for help, the greater danger there is in it for harm if not used or not used properly.

Fire, for instance, is man's greatest friend and worst enemy. Fire can't warm houses, cook food, and rid us of waste material if it does not also have equal power to destroy houses, burn food, and rid us of everything. It must be used properly and for its intended purposes or there will be terrible consequences rather than good results. Improper use of a relatively impotent thing might be inconsequential. Not so with a potent thing, where as much harm is done by improper use, as good is accomplished by its proper use.

When it comes to something as essential as salvation, non-use is abuse. The greater the need for a thing, the more severe are the consequences of not meeting that need.

A physician says he thinks it might be well to let him look into some matter of your health when it is convenient for both of you. That's one thing. On the other hand, when he tells you, "I am admitting you to the hospital right now, and I will call there in a minute to schedule surgery. While I do that, my nurse will call an ambulance for you. It will take you directly to the hospital. Someone from home will have to bring you whatever you need while you are there. You are dropping everything until we get this taken care of. I will cancel the rest of my appointments for today and follow you to the hospital. As soon as we get an opening in the OR, I will start to operate." Now that is obviously a serious matter!

The physician will not carry this out completely against his patient's will. Nor will he force it upon the patient, who still has a legal option. He may and can make the choice to go ahead with the surgery or not.

If you should suffer from having ignored the earlier casual

advice for routine treatment, how should you escape if you ignore the demand for such great surgery? Such is the thought
of the author concerning salvation:

> For if the message spoken by angels was binding, and
> every violation and disobedience received its just punish-
> ment, how shall we escape if we ignore such a great sal-
> vation? (Heb. 2:2, 3, NIV).

The Law of the older covenant wasn't the best the grace of
God did. This epistle opens with a thorough description of how
much superior is the good news in God's Son than the prophetic
judgments and how much greater is the Son than the angels
(chapter 1).

Yet that message declared by angels—the far lesser thing—
was binding upon the people. All who in any way walked across
any of its restrictions suffered the consequences of their sin.

Since that was so under the Old Testament Law, how could
even the simplest-minded child imagine for a moment that
there could possibly be any way that anyone could escape the
consequences of ignoring a salvation so great that it cost the
life of God's Son?

We would not make such a mistake about our physical
health and treat our physician with such despite. Why, then,
do redeemed children of God do this with their spiritual health?

Sin. It's still here, and we are warned about it. The consequence of neglecting to use salvation is that we lose the present
and continuing experience of salvation when we are no longer
being saved from sin.

Salvation cost God the heavenly presence and earthly life of
his Son. The sacrifice brought atonement totally and finally. If
we should neglect such great salvation, we shall not escape the
consequences of that neglect.

People tend to make assumptions about the consequences of
sin and take them too lightly. You may hear such remarks as:
"I'm a sinner anyway; another sin won't change that."—"Better
to sin openly than secretly."—"One more sin won't hurt anymore than it does now."—"Nobody's perfect."—"They're all under the Blood."

Misconceived as these are, more disastrous than these ideas

is the assumption that when eternal destiny is settled, present sins don't matter. "As long as you're going to heaven when you die, sinning some more isn't going to hurt all that much."

It does. All that much.

Perhaps we have done a disservice to people with that trite question: "When you die, can you be sure you're going to heaven?" We mean to hook into something ultimately decisive that is meaningful even to an unsaved person with no present interest in his spiritual condition. "If I can't get him to think about the present, surely I can get him to worry about the end," we might think.

Well enough, if we win the person to Christ and promptly get back to the present where he must begin to live his new life. But those who use the question as a hammer seem content with that. Better, perhaps, to ask, "If you live to be a hundred, are you sure you are alive now?"

For all the Bible says about heaven, the motivation for acceptance of Christ is always to be born again now and actively live a full life from the moment of the second birth. We don't live "spiritual life" from conversion until physical death and then "pass into eternity," and "eternal life."

The life Christ gives is not only everlasting in quantity, but eternal in quality. Spiritual life does have a beginning, although not an end. The New Testament uses the same word for Christ's life as it does for the life he gives to his redeemed children. It is the same life. We are given Christ's own life, which is itself eternal as well as everlasting.

The Christ-life is spiritual and everlasting and eternal—and present. We are in eternity as well as time when we have received eternal life. What we pass into at physical death is the next stage of eternity, not its beginning.

The person who accepted salvation—but neglects to use the salvation he has accepted—is not "being saved." For that person, salvation is not a present experience. The consequence of neglect is the loss of experience.

Careless Christians allow themselves to be deluded about sin. We recall what sin did to us before we became saved from it. "We got through that all right, why not again?" they say. "I can always confess again and get out of it again."

What we recall is the fact of sin and its more obvious evil.

But we were incapable, before we became spiritually alive, of understanding what that sin really did to us. Now, we catch painfully what once escaped us comfortably. We know better now. The days of naive bliss are gone forever.

Call it God's dirty tricks, if you will, but the new birth has spoiled us for a genuine enjoyment of sin. You can never go home to sin again because you have a new home.

I can sin again, but it's not like it used to be. I've lost the real taste for sin. An appetite for sin is still there, and I have gorged myself on sin trying to recapture some of the old satisfaction. But the taste is gone. It's not the same. This very fact is what accounts for some Christians' frantic orgies. They keep hoping one more commission of the sin will bring back the old feeling. But it never does. It's too late.

Sin will not satisfy, but it can become addictive. The Christian's dissatisfaction is the very factor that will drive him to unremitting craving for what used to satisfy. By the time he reasons, even subconsciously, that there will be none, he is addicted and there is no relief.

I used to enjoy telling people off and putting them down. I was really quite "good" at it. I can point to others' scars as my trophies. I'll not claim to be past that sin. But I am encouraged it is not enjoyable any more. In point of fact, seeing people squirm or cower inflicts grievous pain in my heart.

How foolish, when I have also learned a little of the joy and new satisfaction that came on those occasions when I have affirmed and built up!

Sin will never again satisfy; it can never feel good. It is not that a Christian is incapable of reaching the point in spiritual deterioration where sin no longer hurts.

Sin will never again satisfy; but it can come forever to occupy. It can never again feel good; but it can forever numb. The writer of Hebrews called this hardness of heart. But I am learning some sublimations that help.

A person says, "Preacher, that sermon was over my head." What did you say? You would like to say, "But it wasn't over where your head should be!"

But you didn't! But it would've been fun.

Not really. It isn't even as much fun to go through this exercise, but I'll use it as long as it is necessary to save me from the experience of that sin.

We must ingrain into our thinking the understanding that sin will not satisfy. When I contemplate telling someone off, I must say, "Look, Dumb-Dumb, it's not going to help that person—it'll hurt. It's not going to make you feel any better—but worse. It's a lose/lose situation from beginning to end. Forget it."

If I ignore the capability of my great salvation to save me from this immediate sin, I shall not escape the harmful consequences of ignoring the opportunity of being saved from it.

Before going on, I need to lay down a basic principle in regard to the expressions of warnings we find five times in the Epistle to the Hebrews. Don't jump to wild conclusions. Work through to reasonable conclusions.

These warnings in Hebrews are shocking. They are meant to be. Yet they are not unreasonable or outrageous. They make complete sense, and we will value the sense once we grasp it.

We have a tendency to approach threatening things with fears as to what they might say so that we never do learn what they do say. We tend to read things into a statement that were never in the mind of the writer.

I have already pointed out one instance. When I read, "How shall we escape," I must not infer the sentence's direct object. I must not insert into someone else's sentence anything like "hell" or "eternal death." I must, rather, read the direct object that the writer wrote or have a reasonable sense of that which he implies.

I ask, "Escape *what?*" Normal grammar and calm emotions naturally and honestly give the answer: "Escape the consequences." I let the same writer identify and describe the consequences he has in mind. This is easy to do, because what was in his mind when he wrote is what the Holy Spirit put into his mind. The words are his; the teaching is God's.

Although I indicated so in discussion, I didn't make explicit the same conclusion from the first verse.

We read "lest we drift away from *it.*" Here is a pronoun that takes the place of a noun so that the noun does not need to be repeated. Somewhere earlier in the sentence is a noun now repeated by the substitution of a pronoun. To what does *it* refer? Obvious, "What we have heard."

There it is, in the text itself, and in the same sentence. We aren't forced to import a foreign concept to make sense of the text. Why should anyone reach beyond the text and outside Scripture?

Fear. Fear, and not caring as much about what God does say as about what he might say.

Drift away from *salvation*? No, drift away *from what we have heard.*

Escape *hell*? No, escape *the consequences of neglect.*

The verse means we can drift from the experience of salvation by not laying hold daily of salvation doctrine. It means we cannot escape the consequences of neglecting the use of salvation, not experiencing salvation once again.

As we come to the next four warnings, allow the text to speak to us and hear what it says. Then do what it says.

A PERSUASION TO LIVE Hebrews, 2:3b, 4

With this first couplet of exhortation-warning the writer demonstrated the complete picture he created throughout his letter. He laid down the positive exhortation, and built on it the negative warning. Finally, he nailed both down with the results of response to the exhortation and observance of the warning, that is, the persuasion to live the life given.

With a sense of pastoral responsibility, the writer first convinced the reader's thinking and then persuaded behavior. It wasn't enough for him to change his people's minds; they must change their lives. His outline of the gospel's process in coming served as a directive for what is to be done with it.

The first hearing was from "the Lord" himself, that is, Jesus Christ, while he was on earth and preached to crowds and confronted individuals.

Although these first witnesses no doubt repeated what Jesus said, word for word, it isn't the exact verbal repetition he emphasized. As the writer put it, these "confirmed" those words.

The impact of what the initial witnesses said is something like this: "We know Jesus announced this because we heard him announce it. We know it is valid because it is working for us. We witness to what we heard and saw, and testify to what happened to us and through us." The direct testimony of changed lives is the most persuasive of all evidence.

Nothing can be more convincing than the words of Jesus himself. Yet it is the mind that is convinced. A mental concept of theology does not save lives. Logically, what Jesus said is sufficient. Practically, it doesn't quite do it. This, of course, is the result of sin's blinding and hardening.

Most of us need something more than a theory abstract from our experience. We need to see the effectiveness of the reality in lives much like ours.

These readers had met people who had known Jesus and could see the change in their lives because they followed Jesus as his disciples.

The revelation of the gospel was more than the words of Christ and the example of disciples. God himself continued active, in those early apostolic days, with further miracles, referred to also as "signs" and "wonders."

"Signs," the distinctive word of the Apostle John, stresses the indicative nature of miracles. They draw attention to the act and point to its significance. "Wonders" are the "terror things." It is the awesome and breathtaking element of a miracle that strikes terror in the observer.

The generic English word *miracle* translates a word from which is also derived *dynamite, dynamic,* and *dynamo.* "Power" is a good translation.

The signs are promisingly indicative; the wonders are awesomely impressive; and the miracles, powerfully effective. In these, we see demonstrated the power of a saving life.

What about miracles in our lives? If not in what God has done through us or at least to us, surely we have observed such in the lives of some brother or sister nearby. Have we recognized God bearing witness through utilitarian, practical everyday intervention into the usual course of events in order to accomplish his purpose?

Don't look for those demonstrative miracles that were peculiar to turning points in the unfolding of redemptive history. This kind is not a spectacle we need today. When God reflects his glory by the Spirit's transforming an inglorious sinner into the image of his Son, that's a miracle.

When God unaccountably achieves a purpose he was determined to accomplish despite hostile opposition of evil, that's a miracle.

Recognize the miracle. Catch its significance—sign, wonder, or power. Respond to its mandate.

We are persuaded to live spiritually when the Holy Spirit

excites by what he is doing. We want to become part of it. So, too, God persuades us to live by witnessing gifts of the Holy Spirit distributed according to his own will.

He persuades us not to demand certain gifts or any gifts, not to be jealous of gifts in others, or to deny them or to forbid them. We are instead to witness them, praise God for them, and respond to them.

I have been part of congregations who were theologically opposed to emotional excesses. Most of the people sat rigidly defensive, appearing to be against anything the Spirit might wish to do. He never had a chance—not even the Holy Spirit.

We should pray, "Lord, restrain me from all artificial and disruptive demonstration of emotion. Save me from religious deception." We should pray also, "Excite me to all natural and edifying emotional evidence. Free me for spiritual honesty."

To be precise, Christ didn't save our lives when we "were saved." Because of the death of sin, we had no life to be saved. God didn't even give back a lost life. There was no life left to be found by God and returned to us to pick up once again.

God gave us the life of his Son. The lives we live now are not our lives at all. The life is nothing less than the eternal life of God's Son.

The Son himself promises that his leaving the earth bodily would allow his Spirit, when he returned, to indwell all believers. The Spirit could, then, do through all believers "greater works" than Jesus himself could do, confined to one body in one place at a time.

Eternal, spiritual life is more than a thing we have. It is what we do. Existing, like minerals, is not living. Growing, like plants and animals, is not human living. Ultimate life is the activity of a person.

To live a saving life actively is to seek forgiveness for every sin we commit. It is to allow no unforgiven sin in our experience. Salvation is being saved from every sin. Having spiritual life, we can ourselves recognize sin we have committed and freely and immediately confess it, asking the Savior for salvation from that sin also.

To live a saving life actively is to resist the temptation of sin. We could not do this before new birth. We could use social force and resist the moral guilt of some particular acts of sin. Yet we were, by nature, sinners, and sinners can do nothing but sin.

When we recognize the possibility of a sin and actively choose to reject the opportunity, we have been saved from that sin. And this dimension of salvation is greater than the other. To be delivered before the fact is more of salvation than to be redeemed after the fact.

The creative generation of further righteousness comes closer to God's plan for creation than redemptive regeneration from repeated sin. We are convinced that we ought to live actively. Are we also persuaded to do so? Let's move from "oughtness" to action. How do we accomplish this crucial move? *Convince* means to change a mind while *persuade* means to change behavior. If we use the words interchangeably, we confound two distinct realities.

Because the Scriptures present such a convincing case for spiritual living, it is easy to be convinced and to assume behavior will follow. Mental assent and behavioral practice so misconceived become interchangeable in thinking. Then we have a problem. Spiritual qualities are abstract. How can we then know we are actually acting spiritually?

We can do some quantifying, as mentioned in regard to counting the time spent and the frequency of Bible reading, praying, and attendance at worship. Probably every spiritual quality has some tangible expression, some measureable substance. It is indirect, but a helpful procedure. We can get at abstract qualities through their concrete expressions. It's not a matter of certitude, but one of probability.

The procedure is reasonably successful in various fields. Physicians, for instance, don't always know the immediate cause of a particular disease so that it can be treated directly. Yet, there is sometimes a symptom nearly always coincidental with the disease, and experience has shown its treatment usually results in healing of that kind of disease. Some physicians term this "empirical treatment," and others call it "presumptive treatment." They presume upon the presence of a particular type of infection, as an example, in treating rheumatic fever. Taking penicillin to kill that infection usually results in the disappearance of the rheumatic fever.

It is a presumption and not a proof. No harm is done in another regard, and it works.

Are there any kinds of presumptive treatment for spiritual weakness? Possibly.

A middle-aged farmer explained to me how he regained spiritual health. He certainly didn't call it presumptive treatment, but I recognized he knew what he was talking about. His problem, as he and his wife diagnosed it, was his bitter resentment of his wife—and children—and hostility toward them. The most severe symptom was blow-ups when there seemed no connection between what the children were doing and any requirement from the father. He just blew up. Everyone was hurt and frustrated.

He asked his wife to tell him after each blow-up. If they agreed on the incident, he would put a mark on a calendar. At the end of each week, he could count the marks. Few days were unmarked, and many were filled up. It had a vivid impact on his perception. He became convinced of the fact.

Seeing the marks persuaded him to exercise restraint each time he felt anger brewing. Sometimes he had to walk out of the house and kick a dog or two. Then he recognized a nearly exact coincidence between the children's success in school, club, or church on the one hand and bad weather, implement breakdown, or some other farming problem that was his and not theirs on the other. He was jealous and resentful of their success.

The farmer committed himself to praising his family for each success whether he felt happy about it or not. His wife would inform him of the achievements but delay her celebration until Father had a full crack at it. He came to identify with their success and to own it as a second-generation success of his own. After all, he reasoned, they are his children.

The marks on the calendar became fewer and farther between. Each week he determined to outperform and undermark the previous. The more he succeeded one week, the greater his success the next.

The farm problems persisted, but they stayed in the fields and barns. He denied them entrance to his heart and spirit—and home.

This Christian father-farmer witnessed a miracle he could only attribute to the grace of God. This success succeeded in the next. He found himself participating in the miracle.

Eventually but surely, it became less a miracle and more a habit. He was persuaded to live spiritually by acts he chose to perform.

To live a saving life produces. A saving life will be increasingly free of sin.

A saving life will be completing God's creation of a genuine person living an authentic life.

A saving life will be bringing the message of salvation to those lost from it and being the Spirit's instrument of redemption.

A saving life will be exhorting and warning others to live the same kind of life. Convinced we have taken possession of a saved life, now we must also be persuaded to live a saving life.

It has been many years since I learned to secure boats well to their docks. My boats don't drift any more. I am still learning how to lay hold of the things I have heard. My spiritual life doesn't drift as much, either. I am learning to lay hold.

THREE

DO IT, LEST YOU DISBELIEVE

HEBREWS 3:7—4:13

I am on first base and am signaled to steal second. While the pitcher winds up, I am crouched for a quick launch, one foot touching the side of the bag and the other on its way toward second. My eye is on neither the pitcher nor the batter—only second base. One goal: get to second while the ball is moving from pitcher toward batter. I will not leave first until the ball has left the pitcher's hand, and I will be on second before it reaches the catcher's mit and he has time to relay it to the second baseman or shortstop.

Behind me, with eyes focused on the pitcher and quick to follow the ball, is my coach. He controls and will recognize the instant for action. He will command, and I will move.

Too soon and too late would be equally disastrous. On-the-button is the only moment that will do. Timing isn't my worry—only instant obedience.

I am watching neither the game nor even the play since he has that broader view. I fix on second base.

Tense as a finely filed trigger release, I shut out all other sounds. Tuned to the voice of the first-base coach, I hear nothing else.

That voice stabs, "Do it!"

I take off for second, and I don't turn back or slow down. If I fell back now, I'd be tagged out—and that would be the end of the game for me.

This expression, "Do it," has become an especially strong idiom. Although it can be overdone, it comes across as rich and useful. It can only be understood in context, and in context it can never be misunderstood.

It refers to the specific task already assigned. So understood, nothing can be confused with it. There is no need for further explanation.

The verb *do* is the shortest, clearest, and most compelling expression of "function," "act," "perform," or "accomplish."

The verb is imperative—it issues a command.

What is true in that crucial moment of a ball game is more serious at life's critical points. The time comes to do it, and it must be done then.

I like this contemporary idiom, "Do it." I like it for the imperative expressed in the writer's second exhortation: "Do it—lest you disbelieve."

Live what you believe, or you will come to disbelieve what you failed to live. The time comes, the writer urged, to break our preoccupation with the possession of spiritual life and to live that life. We must stop holding on to our lives and start giving them away. Jesus spoke of losing our lives in order to gain them.

Let's quit standing around recognizing God's promises to us, and move to take them. Our focus dare not remain on being a believer. We must believe! The act—not the state! The verb—not the noun!

So, too, we did well to realize a "ministry of presence" has its own validity. Since that concept now seems much to have degenerated into a cop-out from action, recall the earlier understanding. When the Spirit ushers us into the presence of a needy person, it is usually so we can do something for that person. When presence has been adequately celebrated, then, let's catch the need to minister by acts. Ministry is to be present, to be sure, but it is more characteristically a performance in the present. "Let's live spiritual lives and take God's promises or it will become too late and they will be forever gone."

This text presents several strong imperative verbs. All relate to the same idea: "Be careful" (3:12); "Let's fear" (4:1); "Be faithful" (4:2); "Believe" (4:3); "Enter in" (4:3, 6, 10, 11); "Obey" (3:16, 18; 4:6, 11); "Soften hearts" (3:8, 15).

Most versions offer, inadequately, the weak "Be careful." "Take care," or "Care sensitively" grasp the epistle's point. They convey the writer's emphasis upon action beyond being.

"It did not meet with faith in the hearers" (4:2, RSV) implies the need of faithfulness. Perceiving it as a requirement, we say "be faithful." Action is explicit in the words, "faithfully observe." So, too, "soften hearts" positively expresses, "Do not harden your hearts."

Since the command "enter in" refers to entering into an experience, let's put it, "Experience the rest."

All these exhortations, I am convinced, can be summed up as, "Do it."

The time has past, in our Christian lives, to stand and meditate on ideals. Enough celebration of being, for now. It is time to act. Not so much being, but doing is our task.

The sense of urgent immediacy makes itself felt in the epistle's third and fourth chapters. This section (3:7–4:13) presents the second (3:7-19) and third (4:1-13) warnings and ties them together with the second exhortation (throughout the section).

We might think of them in the framework of a time sequence. The second warning draws a lesson from yesterday's failure, and the third describes tomorrow's impossibility. And just as the time between yesterday and tomorrow is today, so between the warnings appears the second exhortation.

By extracting the warnings and exhortations we are finding it easier to focus on the thrust of the epistle's argument. By relating them, we are gaining a perspective on both sides of the coin, that is, the positive and negative.

Most of us have failed sometime in the past. In Israel's case, it was the hardening of their hearts during the wilderness rebellion, which resulted in their being denied entrance into the land of rest.

The author tells his readers—and we are among them— yesterday has already been followed by today. We are to take warning from yesterday's failure, but we are to seize today's opportunity. If you fear now, he said, it's not too late for you.

Tomorrow is final, and we are warned about it. If we do not ourselves enter into the promised rest, we will stumble and not get up.

If we are successfully warned by yesterday's failure, we can do it today. If you hesitate today, be warned that you will come to disbelieve tomorrow. That is an impossible state to fall into.

YESTERDAY'S FAILURE Hebrews 3:7-19

In the more distant yesterday, the people, called Hebrews of the nation called Israel, failed. In the recent past, Hebrew-like readers failed. To our own sorrow and grief, spiritual failure is a characteristic part of the yesterdays of most.

This reminder of failure should insure that it remains yesterday's tragedy and does not invade today to destroy its opportunity. It is a warning.

Don't be unbelieving "Hebrews," the writer warned. Such resist when the going gets tough and fail to enter into the promise.

The Israelites in Egypt had finally learned to trust Moses as God's messenger and as their leader. As they escaped the pursuing Egyptian army, that trust spoiled into an arrogant self-confidence and hostile contempt toward God and his servant.

Rather than being humble and grateful, they became proud and dissatisfied. Having escaped the bondage of Egypt, they also lost its bounty. They suffered hunger. Whereas the Red Sea was once a barrier to be removed, they had gone too long without seeing water. They became thirsty. God had given the commandments, but they had their own way of doing things. They became defiant. Although they heard God speak to them through the man who alone had stood "face to face with God," they demanded to be heard. They became rebellious.

The Hebrews wanted to eat the manna of the exodus and have the onions of bondage, too. They wanted God's deliverance and indulgence, both in the same package. We want to be saved from the guilt of sin, but have fun with sin too.

Some of the testimonies of salvation I hear sound more like bragging about how smart one was to have hung it up just in time along with a vicarious reliving of the good ol' days.

In reaction to the Hebrews' rebellious trend—later becoming an incorrigible rebellion—God was to prohibit them from entering into the land of rest. These died still in the wilderness between Egypt and Canaan. The writer grieved that anything similar should happen to his people, and we can be frightened that it might happen to us. It might, and this is how it begins.

It did not take until apostolic times, of course, for this analogy to be recognized or this parallel lesson to be preached. The writer developed it most thoroughly, but he quoted throughout this section from Psalm 95:7-11.

The heart of the quotation is the oath: "They shall never enter my rest" (v. 11). He cited it three times (3:11; 4:3, 5).

Hebrews' second warning is "Do not harden your hearts as in the rebellion" because God was forced to swear, "They shall never enter my rest" and had to report that "they were unable to enter because of unbelief."

The Hebrews of Israel missed God's rest because of their rebellion, and the "Hebrews" of any age are warned. If man's rebellion is repeated, so will be God's rejection.

The events of Numbers were, he said, "the day of testing in the wilderness." The faith God required of his chosen people was altogether reasonable because it could have been built upon the results of a test. He led the people to where they "put me to the test and saw my works for forty years."

When the embarrassment of refusing to accept test results was too severe, they alternated by refusing to put God's promises to the test. Whatever device they were using at the moment, "They always go astray in their hearts" because "they have not known my ways." It could be no different.

The author makes good use of scriptural tradition when he presses the figure of hard hearts. They were callously insensitive to healthy appeal.

Isaiah's commission to make hearts hard (Isa. 6:10), because not many would believe the proclamation he was to give (53:1), was used by the Apostle John as the prophetic prelude to the final ministry of Jesus. Because the Jews of that day "would not believe in him" (John 12:37), it came to be "they could not believe" (v. 39). If a man is not willing to believe when he is able—Isaiah was told and John learned—he will not be able when he is willing.

The Greek words, *sklerunete tas kardia* even sound like modern medicine's "cardiac sclerosis," a term which refers to the closing of the arteries of the heart so that blood cannot pass through them. The Greek words here picture a calloused heart that cannot sense stimuli.

The ancients envisioned the heart being so often pricked that scar tissue has formed. The heart no longer felt what it once felt keenly. Conscience is restructured so that, worse than being useless, it becomes deceptive.

What hardens hearts? Men, the writer said, harden their own hearts. He used expressions such as "go astray in their hearts," "not known my ways," "unbelieving heart," "hardened by the deceitfulness of sin," "rebellion," "disobedient."

God also, the writer says, hardens men's hearts. "I was angry with that generation. . . . So I declared an oath in my anger, 'They shall never enter my rest.'"

You can take the psychological description of the mental-emotional process by which men choose to reject what God has offered. Or you can take the theological explanation by which God decides to prohibit a man from ever receiving the offer he has rejected.

The authentic offer that could have been received as a fulfilled promise is changed to a final prohibition. Man does his part, but in the final analysis God has his way. In prophetic perspective, God is ultimately responsible for everything that occurs in history.

No man successfully mocks God. His Word will not return to him without having accomplished its purpose (Isa. 55:11). If it does not soften hearts to repentance because of the sinner's obstinance, it will harden them because of God's justice. But the Word of God, just because it is God's Word, must and will do something. The same sun that melts wax hardens clay, depending upon the response of the material.

The presumptuous sinner's obstinate refusal to accept God's offer is but one side of the coin. The other is God's sovereign withdrawal of his offer. Far from being an inconsistency, it is perfect justice.

When God speaks to me and I do not wish to hear, I refuse to listen. If God speaks more loudly to overcome my refusal to listen, I begin to build defenses so I cannot hear. While I am powerless to still the voice of God, I have the ability to dull my own hearing. If I should then ever want to hear, I would be unable. When I have so corrupted God's creation of a sensitive human being, God stops speaking in my direction. In point of fact, God speaks against me.

Any one of us is capable of so dulling our ears that we cannot hear God and so hardening our hearts that we cannot feel him. It has happened before, and it will happen again.

If, however, you still feel something when God approaches, it is what this epistle calls "today." It is still time to do something about it.

As you read this now, the Holy Spirit may stab you with the conviction of some specific sin in your life. I don't need to know what the sin is. It is the Spirit who brought it to your mind as you read about it. If this still hurts, there is hope. You become uncomfortable, and you are right that you cannot live with it for long.

You will either let God remove the sin that hurts or you will remove the hurt that signals sin. Either guilt will be removed by God's forgiveness or the feeling of guilt will be covered by your hardness of heart.

Whether in reading this book or hearing a sermon or thinking about ourselves, whenever we feel guilt and conviction it is "today" and today is the day of repentance.

We dare not put it off until tomorrow because tomorrow is impossible. When it arrives, we will no longer know what it is that bothered us in what by then will have become yesterday.

We must not tolerate for another moment any straying of heart, any ignoring of God's ways, any unbelief, any hardening, any deceitfulness, any rebellion, or any disobedience. You and I know what to do. Let's do it. Let us act on our belief and enter into what we believe.

This epistle, as all the Bible, is thoroughly honest about history. Here is the example of heroes of the faith (chapter 11). Here, too, is the instructive example of faithless cowards.

We sing, "Faith of our fathers," yes, but not all fathers were faithful. Their story must also be studied and for the same purpose, although requiring different action.

Another difference emerges here. We emulate the faithful only by choice and effort; the faithless are duplicated without either. Therein lies the danger. The precedent has been set.

We will repeat in our experience what they had in theirs. They have left us a miserable inheritance. It will be this way unless we take steps to make it different.

For a long while, as pastor and counselor, I was puzzled about the scandalous repetition of bad marriages from one generation to another. I would counsel with a boy concerning his parents' terrible marriage and find he understood well what ruined it. This is one boy, I would think, who will either insure he has the right girl to marry or never marry at all. Inevitably, he not only created as bad a marriage as his parents, but chose precisely the same unsuitable kind of girl.

I finally applied to marriage plans what I had known in other areas. For good or for bad, we tend to duplicate in our lives whatever it is that was in our parents'. We feel traitors to the family to reject family values—even unacceptable values. We seem to feel we have no right to have a better marriage than our parents.

Moral and spiritual failure becomes a family tradition. It is a habit—even a comfortable habit. We expect to fail, and we meet our expectations. Add to the spiritual failure of the past generation, the failure of our parents. Add to that the failure of our peers and, to that, our own past failure. What a sum! Many have a precedent that goes back several generations and into all neighboring camps.

What about good families, in which the precedent is of the good? Parents are responsible to create that heritage. Children are obliged to capitalize on it. While I find it difficult to overstate the strength of this value, I also worry about that principle: the bad exerts a more severe impact than the influence of good. Choice is still essential.

While it is relatively easy to choose ownership of family good, the choice must still be made. When we make no choice and exercise no effort, drifting begins. Unless we lay hold of what we have been taught, our families' weakest qualities will influence more than their best.

Man has been so infected by the Fall that, while still in the process of redemption and with sanctification incomplete, humanity sustains this frightful vulnerability.

If we are not growing, we are degenerating. Children can merely duplicate the spirituality of their parents for a limited time. If they don't grow beyond where parents started them, they will fall back behind it.

Each generation must be stronger than the one from which it learned. This is an exhortation the writer of Hebrews keeps pressing.

We will fail—unless we take this warning and accept this exhortation. There is nothing we need do in order to repeat the experience of the Hebrews. There is much we must do to avoid it. But there are many things we can do about it.

All those failures in the wilderness? Surely, those must have been pagans. We can expect such to have been the reaction of the initial readers. I anticipate this reaction from Christians who read today. Surely, some hope, it is the unsaved referred to here—not people actually born-again. No, it was the Hebrews, members of the covenant chosen for the land promised. It was they who disbelieved and failed to enter in.

Does nervousness about the doctrine of eternal security rise again? Of course. As we read these things, we wonder if the writer believed in the doctrine. He did, but we'll not catch it here because he says nothing about it.

Be patient. To the Calvinists, I say, "I hear you, and I settled that long ago." To the Arminians, I say, "I've finally figured out what you've been trying to tell me all these years. Let's climb to the full perspective and breathe the air from up there."

Numbers narrates the story of Hebrews who actually were saved from Egyptian bondage and really experienced a journey. But they did not enter in to the promise. Hebrews reminds latter day "Hebrews" they (we), too, will repeat the experience unless they do something about it.

"So we see that they were unable to enter because of unbelief."

Let's not be like those unbelieving Hebrews. They rebel when the going gets tough. They fail to enter into the promise.

TODAY'S OPPORTUNITY Hebrews 4:1-10

So much for yesterday. It is done, and that's the way it must remain. It has been worth this much consideration as a warning not to repeat.

Today is where it's at. It is where we are, and it is where and when we act. If yesterday meant failure, today means opportunity.

Is your heart still sensitive to what God is saying? Can you hear him speak and feel him press? Then it's still today. There's still hope. While it is still today for you, act in faith to experience all God has promised. That is the way to accomplish life.

Life is not a punishment to be endured or yet a task to be completed. Life is God's gift. It is a creation to be accomplished.

Yet the Israelites just could not bring themselves to trust God to the point of trying him. The rest ahead was more acceptable as a promise than an experience.

The standard explanation is obvious. They feared the Canaanites more than they trusted God. They knew the Canaanites were stronger than they and could defeat them in any attempted invasion. About God and his promise, they weren't so sure.

How could they doubt God's power to defeat the chaotic tribes of Canaan when he had so dramatically demonstrated his absolute power over the well-organized and keenly disciplined army of Egypt? Did they really doubt God has the power to fulfil his promise?

Possibly, but probably not. Perhaps they doubted God's willingness more than his ability. He could give the land to them, but would he? After all, why should he? Such unmerited favor wasn't at all like their thinking. "Suspect such a generous offer. You can't trust it," they may have thought.

Even a doubting of God's willingness may not yet be the answer. They should have seen that God was going to astounding lengths to follow through on his promise, which wouldn't have been reasonable if he didn't mean to keep it.

If neither God's ability nor his willingness were distrusted, what then? If God could insert them into the land and if he would do so, the thing to fear must be just that. He might keep his promise—and what then?

If Israel had entered in it could no longer run for protection by one neighbor against another but would need to protect itself against all its neighbors. Worse, there would be no one to trust but God.

God would no longer drop manna on the ground, and the people would need to cultivate and harvest plants.

They could no longer feel sorry for themselves but would be called upon to show compassion on others.

They would lose all excuses for failure and would forever be expected to be at their best.

I am not as sure of the collective fears of a nation as I am of individuals. I don't want to appear overly certain of Israel's motivation, but I think I do understand how the epistle's readers—and how we—react to such contingencies.

If we enter into what God has promised; we are always on the spot, and there is no letting up. We are conspicuous, and there's no place to hide. We've blown the excuse that we are unworthy of God's favor because we've now proved God's favor has nothing to do with our worthiness but only his grace and our belief.

A great number of Christians seem to be more afraid of success than failure. Failure we know well. We know its ins and outs, its comings and goings. Failure is predictable, familiar, and even has a comfort about it.

But success and victory? Those are utterly new experiences, and they are frightening. Many of us would rather tough it through with familiar failure than confront strange success.

Athletes have performed with promising skill until the last event and then failed to do for the final time what they had often done before. Young painters have almost completed a picture and then destroyed it just when they could have finished. Logic cannot account for this.

Sometimes we don't know what to do with spiritual victory. How do we act when we have been victorious? What do we say? Worse, what demands does this make upon us? If we succeed in something, won't God and man expect even more from us? Are we really willing to pay the cost of continued spiritual victory? What pressure that puts us under!

Other teenagers at our Bible camp in Round Lake, Illinois, broke the rules and went out after hours. When our pastor found me in the cottage, he said, "Thank God, you're still here. You're a good boy, Wallace."

I was pleased to have my pastor's approval until I realized he would now always expect me to observe rules. If ever I also wanted the fun of rule-breaking, too much would be expected of me. I could now never get away with it.

When we fail to do what is necessary to succeed, added to the pain of our loss is the humiliation of the failure itself. Since we have already failed, we seek to excuse it by claiming success now to be impossible. We prove the impossibility by creating it through the destruction of the possible. At this we succeed, and now it really and finally is impossible.

If we fail to succeed, we succeed at failure. If we refuse to do what is possible, we destroy all possibility to do anything.

But God always has the last laugh. Christian believers may prefer failure and forego success and exercise that option. Nonetheless, as the Righteous Judge and Sovereign Lord bangs down his gavel for the final time on individual cases, he announces, "They shall never enter my rest. You have made the choice I allowed you. Now I shall enforce your choice so it is no longer yours, but my ultimate judgment."

In quoting Psalm 95:11, the writer presented this statement as it is there. Neither a prediction of probability nor an announcement of divine intent, it is an oath of prohibition enforced by God himself. The Hebrew word used is a prosaic expression, but the highly literary Greek of the epistle seems to use a contemporary idiom in shortened form. The full oath is likely to have been something like, "If they shall enter my rest, I am not God!"

If a Christian should refuse to enter into the promised rest when God allows him, God will not allow him though he should come to seek it.

We have been thinking about "rest" without defining it. While the author doesn't define, he describes by the use of two figures.

Rest means arrival at one's destiny, as Israel journeyed from Egypt through the Sinai desert and arrived at Canaan. Rest also means the completion of one's work, as God created the world in six days and rested on the seventh.

How eager—no, anxious—many modern Christians are to take "rest" in the sense of doing nothing. It means, as these figures make clear, anything but that. It is dynamic and active. Entering into the land is followed by occupying the land. Completion of creation is followed by working the creation. The preliminaries are over. Real life begins. Graduation, someone reminds every June, is the beginning and not the end. We are graduated to the main business. It is a commencement of life work.

To put the figures together, God's rest is being in complete fellowship with God and current in spiritual maturation. Not maturity, but maturing. The measurements of maturity progress as we grow so that we must always be maturing. The moment a thing is fully mature, it begins to rot.

We are always entering into the land of promise. We are always being creative with God's creation. Canaan, of course, is the geographical symbol of God's promise. On this, too, we need to correct careless assumptions of shallow thinking.

Canaan, in the Bible, is never a picture of heaven. And so, crossing the Jordan River is never a picture of death and passing from earth to heaven.

From whence, then, the colorful figures? Negro spirituals, not the Bible. There was a time when American Blacks were so hopelessly enslaved that what God had promised to all peoples could not be conceived of as a reality anywhere, anytime on this earth. If a rest remained to the slaves, it must be "yonder in the sweet bye-and-bye."

However socially understandable, the slaves were theologically wrong. No excuse remains now to ignore the biblical figures and adopt folk songs as the basis for doctrine. Canaan—the land of promise—is here and now. It is earthly reality here and now, not heavenly bliss then and there!

We should despair less of sin's corruption, and hope more in Christ's redemption. The Savior can so deliver from sin and transform character that we can change the world around us by the influence of redeemed lives and the accomplishment of redeeming acts.

God created earth for man, and he put man here to enjoy it. For a believer to become so spiritually and morally discriminating that he can actually find enjoyment on this earth—even in the midst of sin and evil—is one of salvation's grandest achievements.

We don't need to wait until the Lord takes us from earth or until he returns to it in order to inherit the promise. It is here and now. But we do need to enter in and take possession.

The reason many Christians find hope only in heaven is they have refused the hope that is set before them. That's what the Hebrews did, and that's where they dropped dead.

We must not be like them.

> Good news came to us just as to them; but the message which they heard did not benefit them, because it did not meet with faith in the hearers. . . . Since therefore it remains for some to enter it, and those who formerly re-

ceived the good news failed to enter because of
disobedience (Heb. 4:2-6, RSV).

There is no need to repeat the miserable mistakes of anyone
before our time. On the contrary, we must refuse those mistakes and go on to greater things. If we follow those for whom
things were spiritually great, our spiritual experience must be
greater still.

There is no father who is so successful as he who is out-
stripped by his son. The best mother is she who rears a better
daughter. The children who most honor their parents are those
who do the most with what the parents invested in them.

We are entitled to as much spiritual maturity as our parents
enjoyed. We are obliged to exceed even that.

Here is the best place to begin, and now the best time.

For many years I thought about losing excess weight. One of
the several games I played was to wait for the most dramatic
time, which would then become nostalgic for me, a Day of Re-
membrance.

Or I would wait for the most effective time to begin dieting.
After Thanksgiving is a good time. But, then, Christmas comes
so soon after that. And New Year's after that. Easter, too. And
vacation . . . and . . .

One day I realized the best time to begin dieting is today.
Waiting until the chocolate cake is finished is counter-
productive.

I made a decision that I would lose weight.

I made a commitment that I would eat wisely.

I don't know when I started other than it was then called
today. It was about six months prior to my weighing sixty
pounds less than I had for years. At nine months, I had lost a
total of seventy pounds.

No secrets. No tricks. Just reasonable success, rationally
pursued.

Success = decision + commitment.

Today, decide to enter into what God has promised. Commit
yourself to keep entering in. That is spiritual success. It's God's
promise.

We commit two exceedingly common mistakes when making

spiritual decisions. We promise too much, and we promise too long.

A young husband vowed in my study, "Pastor, for the rest of my life I am going to read the Bible for one hour every day and every day pray another hour for all the missionaries. I'm going to lead one person to Christ every week I live."

I tried to negotiate: "Why don't you commit yourself to reading from the Bible five minutes each day this week? Pray for only your family as you drive to the shop each morning. Sometime during the week, speak to one person about Christ. At the end of this excitingly productive week, come back and let's plan the next week."

That wasn't dramatic enough for him. He was going to do great and mighty things that we knew not but he knew certainly. He never made it through the second day.

We have much to learn from the effectiveness of Alcoholics Anonymous. One of their principles is, "Live for today. Never promise what you are going to do tomorrow. Just commit yourself for today to today."

Experienced AA counselors refuse to tolerate such rash statements as "I promise I'll never take another drink as long as I live!"

"That's too much," they insist. "How about today? What are you going to do today?"

"Well, I will not take a drink today."

That's it.

"If I get through today without drinking, what about tomorrow?"

Tomorrow will never come. It will always be today. And every today you will say the same thing: "Today I will not drink. I don't know about tomorrow, only today."

We go through your life that way. And every day will be today, and every today will be successful. We must not promise God fantastic things we are going to do tomorrow. We must decide what ordinary things we will do today, then commit ourselves to them—today.

"There remains a sabbath rest for the people of God."

It's ours.

If our hearts still have some sensitivity to God's encouragement, we can act. But we must act today so we can experience all he has promised. As we do this, we accomplish life.

TOMORROW'S IMPOSSIBILITY Hebrews 4:11-13

Spiritual failure is a part of the past for so many! Opportunity today exists for everyone! Tomorrow holds the impossibility of recovering from yesterday's failure or taking advantage of today's opportunity. The task of doing it, in the figure of the writer, is always for today. As long as we are doing it today, this kind of tomorrow will never descend upon us.

Today, we must work as hard as we can to do everything that has been given us to do to enter into God's promises. If we fail to work today, the Living Word himself will deny us God's blessings.

The third warning of the Epistle to the Hebrews occurs at this point. The second, shortly before (3:7–4:1), is a warning about missing God's rest:

> Do not harden your hearts as in the rebellion. . . . "They shall never enter my rest." . . . They were unable to enter because of unbelief. . . . Let us fear lest any of you be judged to have failed to reach it.

The fourth—more than a mere missing, a personal failure—is a warning of the disqualification from entering the rest:

> That no one fall by the same sort of disobedience. . . . For the Word of God is living and active. . . . And before him no creature is hidden.

A decision-making man hardens his heart psychologically. A sovereign God hardens the man's heart metaphysically. The sinner who will not believe, cannot believe.

The spiritual traveler who fails to enter into the land of promise will be prevented from entering by the Son of God himself.

The third warning is: "Let us, therefore, strive to enter that rest."

No stronger word for this action existed in the vocabulary of a Greek writer. Such English expressions as "endeavor" and "give diligence" are most common in the various versions of the several places the word occurs throughout the epistles.

The word carries the sense of a command to do thoroughly everything within your power upon every factor under your control, using every resource you can lay your hands on, to effect all that is humanly possible. American language is colored by such idioms as "Leave no stone unturned"; "Exhaust every possibility"; and "Hold nothing back, and give it everything you have."

This exhortation to self-effort flies in the face of religious people who feel the most a person may do is perform a ceremony that allows God to do the rest for them.

It flies also in the face of artificially pious people who feel finite, and sinful man can do nothing of spiritual merit and everything must be left to God.

The former misconception is understandable since God has, especially in the Old Testament, prescribed religious ceremonies. It is easy to forget these symbols affected the worshiper who performed them rather than the God who observed.

The latter is understandable since God has, especially in the New Testament, proclaimed the Spirit's power. It is easy to forget the Holy Spirit does his work within and through the believer, whose temple he is.

Balanced understanding comes from appreciating the cooperation between the omnipotent Lord and his impotent creatures. In ourselves, we are nothing, but in Christ we enjoy the hope of glory.

The person who claims he has the ability to accomplish things of ultimate spiritual value by native ability betrays outrageous arrogance. The one who doubts God and claims he does them by lordship of his own creation blasphemes. Things we can do to enter into the rest lie before us because God created them for us to do when he created humanity. When he created us individually, God invested in his children the ability to do them.

Though I cannot create a flower, I can plant seed. If I fail to plant the seed given to me, God will not stick the flower in the ground to cover my failure.

I cannot prevent obscene sexual thoughts from entering my

mind when I see a sexually provocative woman. I can relate to her as a person and love her as my sister so that thinking of her as a sex object is rendered at least difficult. I can so practice total love for my wife and so celebrate through sexual relations that this sex experience crowds out empty fantasies.

We may not be able to take spiritual initiative, but we can respond to the Spirit's initiative. We cannot grow the fruit of the Spirit, but we can cultivate the ground in which the Spirit grows fruit. And we must.

We are creatures of faith, to be sure. We are redeemed by our faith in God's grace, and we so live by faith. Such faith is an active practice and not a passive possession. Faith is not so much something we have, but something we do.

We aim prayer wrong when we plead "Give me more faith." We hit the target by asserting "Help me to use the faith you have given."

As we review the Book of Numbers, we read of complaining cries and rebellious acts. It forms the theme from Egypt to Sinai. Yet, the Israelites were not then, or for that cause, disqualified. God was tolerant with those failures, and it is not those to which the author refers in the Epistle to the Hebrews.

Those were, so to speak, benign outbursts of juvenile protest. They had just begun the journey, and God had not yet given them the Commandments and attendant instructions. He had not yet proved himself in terms of the promised land itself.

It was when Israel was encamped at Kadesh-Barnea and received the report of the spies. All before had been preparation for this. It had taken but two years to move from Egypt to the Sinai revelation and on to the gateway to Canaan. Now was the time to enter into the land and take possession of what had been promised and is now offered. God said, "Do it."

But they didn't. Theirs was no simple failure, but an accomplishment of will—not an inability, but a refusal. Israel's childish unbelief hardened into adult disbelief. The ancient Hebrews died in the wilderness, not because of unbelief and protest freshly out of Egypt but disbelief and rebellion when finally at Kadesh-Barnea.

There is a fundamental difference between unbelief and disbelief. The former is simple and naive, while the latter is sinister and profound.

Unbelief can be as innocent as an inability, real or imagined, to believe. Or ability can be recognized, but the unbeliever is timid about exercising it. Carelessness about the opportunity to believe is sometimes the cause.

Unbelief, then, is a simple lack of belief. It is passive. Disbelief, on the other hand, is distinctly active. It is not an accidental weakness, but a constitutionally strong belief. This is a belief against trust. It is a refusal to believe that which one knows full well can and must be believed.

Unbelief is a failure; disbelief, a choice.

A Christian who is in unbelief is in danger. If he tolerates unbelief, it will become an embarrassment to himself and an offense against God. The unbelief becomes persistent in reaction. Persistent unbelief hardens into determined disbelief. Chronic disbelief becomes incorrigible. Such a person loses the belief he had and cannot again believe.

No enemy of the gospel is so bitter and hostile as that one. Admitted into God's family by rebirth as a child, he has chosen to disbelieve against the faith he once enjoyed. He can flee the house, but his birth remains an unchangeable fact. He acts a stranger from home, but exists homeless.

Every Christian eventually stands at that place in his spiritual journey which is, to him, a personal Kadesh-Barnea. Long ago, he was delivered from the bondage of sin by Christ. The Spirit set him out upon the journey by carrying him through the bland and drab spaces of juvenile ignorance and naivete. Then he cajoled through the seasoned and tinted reaches of adolescent confusion and doubts. The young Christian had but heard of the rich and brilliant heights of adult understanding and wisdom. Along the journey, he had received from on high the commandments for holy living and fellowship with God.

Now he stands at the gateway to the territory promised and toward which everything has been directed. A decision is demanded. Following must be a commitment. When we stand at this place and face this moment, we see the scenery of Kadesh-Barnea. Ahead, if we enter in, is Canaan and its bright promises.

Behind, if we refuse, is the wilderness and its grim realities.

Unbelief is no longer tolerated. It must ripen to the active belief of commitment or it will harden to the hostile disbelief of rebellion. No middle ground. The alternatives are these alone.

We cannot wait idly until heaven opens to us and then pick up where we left off, having skipped this stage. To try is to find ourselves, as others before, wandering in circles about a dry, scorching land-of-nothing until we drop.

If we think we can put off the critical decision and enter in eventually, look at who stands guarding the gateway:

> For the word of God is living and active, sharper than any two-edged sword, piercing to the division of soul and spirit, of joints and marrow, and discerning the thoughts and intentions of the heart. And before him no creature is hidden, but all are open and laid bare to the eyes of him with whom we have to do (4:12, 13, RSV).

Application to the Bible as the Word of God is obvious. The message of the Scriptures convicts of sin with devastating impact. The threat here is greater still. People have managed to escape the conviction of the Bible. One can ignore it, unopened on a shelf. Or one can read, even study, unmoved by its message. The Bible has been successfully patronized as an anthology of children's tales and dismissed as a pack of cultic myths. But we must ultimately deal not with a book but a Person.

In John 1, the term "Word of God" refers immediately and basically to the Son of God, who was in the beginning with God and is God. The Bible is the written word expressing, in the words of men, the Living Word who is the self-expression of the Godhead.

In addition to the usual sense of the term, the text displays itself clearly. Its pronouns, immediately following the noun, are personal. The Word of God is in the masculine gender. No creature is hidden "before him," and the Word of God is spoken of as "him with whom" we have to do.

The ancient Hebrews were caught on geographic display so that even undiscerning bystanders could observe whether they moved on northward into Canaan or turned back southward to the desert.

The reluctant but deceptive modern Hebrew hopes he can exploit the peculiar nature of his setting, which is immaterial and nonvisual. Since his movement is moral and spiritual, he pretends by his social and religious expressions. The decision is internal, and a well rehearsed public profession covers.

He is a talented social actor and a skillful religious shaman. He deceives others and, sometimes, himself.

But we are neither accountable to nor judged by humans. The Son of God, like a two-edged sword, pierces through every layer of defense and cuts between every chunk of pretense. No one who disbelieves will enter into the land of promise. The Son of God himself is there to see to that.

Can there be a more grievous warning than this? Jesus, the priest who understands our every feeling, is he who also knows our every motive. He is both Judge and Savior, Guard and Lord.

This is why we must work as hard as we can to do everything that is ours to do. Results—not profession—will be measured. We enter not by our invasion, but the Word's acceptance. Not by the number of things we do, but we are judged by the belief we have experienced and the faith we have exercised.

And the Son of God knows. There is no fooling him. The Living Word himself will deny to us God's blessings if we disbelieve them. If we will not choose to enter into what is promised, he will see to it that we cannot. It can get that bad, but it need not be so. What we need to do, we can do today.

FOUR

GO ON, LEST YOU DISBELIEVE

HEBREWS 5:11—6:20

Children succeed in riding bicycles when they set themselves to moving ahead. Hesitation causes them to fall. Momentum creates the balance that not only protects them from falling but assures they get somewhere.

For a similar reason, we should go on in our spiritual growth. Standing still, being satisfied with what we now have, is no option because we can't really do that. We either go on or we fall back. The falling back, in that case, would be no accident. We would have chosen to fall.

If we fail to go on, we lose the gain we once had. If we lose much for long, we throw ourselves in danger of never recovering from the loss. We just must go on.

"Therefore," the writer exhorts, "let us leave the elementary teachings about Christ and go on to maturity—" (6:1). He also warns that it is impossible to restore again to repentance (6:4) those who know the facts fully and then commit apostasy.

Of the five warning/exhortation sections in the Epistle to the Hebrews, this is the classic. That is to say, the writer states the case simply and balances warnings and exhortations evenly. He first confronts us with a problem (5:11—6:3), spiritual childishness. He warns (6:4-8) about unrestorable falling. He lifts us with a characteristic exhortation (6:1, 2, 9-20), encouragement from the past.

PROBLEM: SPIRITUAL CHILDISHNESS *Hebrews 5:11—6:3*

Christians who content themselves with remaining in the early stage of spiritual growth, we have seen, are in danger. Childhood quickly degenerates into childishness.

Baby food that adequately nourishes the newborn becomes seriously inadequate for the growing youth. So, too, a Christian cannot subsist on spiritual baby food for long before he becomes undernourished and then malnourished.

He neither desires adult, body-building food nor could he digest it if he ate it. Unable to understand deeper truths of spiritual reality, he can't experience the richer elements of spiritual life.

This truth forced the writer of Hebrews to pause in his discourse. Not at all turning aside from his principal appeal, he intensified it here. The pause comes in the specific illustration he attempted.

He began to make his point about the ultimacy of Christ's priesthood and its atonement by illustrating with the unique priesthood of Melchizedek.

He began to set up the analogy (4:14–5:9) and got as far as showing that Christ was "designated by God to be high priest in the order of Melchizedek" (v. 10), and stopped. "We have much to say about this, but it is hard to explain because you are slow to learn" (v. 11). I am painfully aware, we can hear him sigh, this is heavy stuff for you because you're not ready for it.

He refuses to allow them to escape what they need, nonetheless, and gets back to it later (6:20). The section before us, the fourth warning and third exhortation, is actually a parenthesis inserted into the Melchizedek analogy. The immediate problem is the inability of the readers to comprehend the argument the writer has started. It was symptomatic of the ultimate problem. Just as they were unable to think through Christian theology, they were unable to work through the Christian life. Their inability to grasp the concept resulted from their failure to lay hold of the promise. They couldn't think deeply because they had settled for shallow lives.

The writer, an effective communicator, slowed down to where his readers were currently responding. A responsible pastor-teacher, he led them on from there. That he should be forced still to lead and teach these people is a crime. "For though by this time you ought to be teachers, you need someone to teach you again the first principles of God's word."

Picture the writer in a kindergarten classroom leaning over to look into the eyes of adult-size bodies scrunched behind tiny desks and smothering stools that threaten to collapse under the weight of self-indulgent obesity. Ignored on the floor are elementary and high school textbooks, and stuffed thoughtlessly into them are blank admission certificates and tuition credits for college.

Down the hallway are teacherless classrooms with students running wild. The missing teachers are here. Still kindergartners, they ask "Teacher, tell us again what comes after ABC. We forget."

The Lord urged us to be "childlike" (Matt. 18:2, 3), but not "childish." To become childlike is a form of growth, as it means we have become teachable. But emotional and social childishness is a tremendous problem in our society. Spiritual and moral childishness is a monstrous problem in our churches and families. The behavior of many older people involves the act of a child costumed in adult motions and language. It's a social game. We all know the rules and cover each other by pretending we don't notice lest someone blow our cover in retaliation.

The biggest difference between real children and childish adults is that children are honest and trustworthy, even when they lie and deceive. Children tend to tell lies and make deceptions with built-in disclaimers. They tell a lie and let you know it's a lie.

Childlikeness promises; childishness destroys.

Destructive spiritual childishness frustrated the writer's teaching and angered his spirit.

> You need milk, not solid food! Anyone who lives on milk, being still an infant, is not acquainted with the teaching about righteousness. But solid food is for the mature, who by constant use have trained themselves to distinguish good from evil (5:12-14).

The contrast of baby food and table food is how we would discuss it in the modern idiom. You sit in a high chair and are spoon-fed baby food, when you should be sitting up at the table and eating your own food.

Worse than simply preferring elementary teaching, the people addressed here actually needed it since they had done little with what they had received earlier and this was actually all they could take.

Hamburgers and hotdogs are the universal fare of children. There's just something convenient about a hotdog. It bites apart so easily and slips down with no effort at all. When our children were small and unknowing, I was glad they liked hotdogs, since it allowed us adults to have more expensive, solid food. One day, however, our older son announced with a smile, "I think I'll try a steak today."

If we had tried to force steak on him before, he would have had none of it. You have to cut steak up into stupid, bitsy pieces. And a little guy would wreck his jaw with all that chewing. Besides, you have to think about a steak to catch the flavor.

Our Christian circles have far too many hotdog kids and not nearly enough steak-loving adults.

Some people never learn. The longer one refuses solid spiritual food, the less likely it is he will ever try it. That fact worried the writer of Hebrews.

Every September, in the years I taught freshman survey in a Bible college, I saw the same trick enacted by still another entering class. The volunteer for class devotions would say, "Let us turn in our Bibles, if you brought them with you, to Hezekiah 42:18." He and others like him who had played this game in youth groups for years, smiled while a few frantically flipped pages in their Bibles looking for such a book.

The class probably couldn't have found Habakkuk very easily and, surely, couldn't expound it. The ones who got caught were typically recently saved believers. Wounded and frightened, they confess fears about keeping up with the old Christians who have gone to Sunday school all their lives. But these are usually the ones who try hardest and eventually make progress. The others, trusting in what they knew, grew very little.

And so it was. It always is. So it is that a scandalous number of youth from "good Christian homes" end up enslaved by the cults. And I do mean end up since even most who are eventually deprogramed are rendered nothings. The cult having been discredited, it still looks too much like the uncreditable form of religion they had suffered, which drove them to the cult.

What little nourishment is found by the spiritually immature is like strained vegetables, which slip down effortlessly. Those fed by the cults have only precooked fast foods jammed down their throats.

The spiritually mature have grown, and continue to grow, on fresh staples that they themselves have harvested.

To grow beyond childishness one has to remain childlike in order to keep growing toward maturity, which the writer of Hebrews described as being experienced "in the word of righteousness" (5:13, RSV).

The writer recognized the immature believers to be lacking in experience with the demands of righteousness. His word was elsewhere used for being tempted, in the negative sense, or tried, in the positive sense. The mature are those who have responded to the demands of righteousness and have become thoroughly acquainted with them through that experience.

A young executive was said to be seeking the counsel of the retiring bank president he was about to replace.

"Sir, how can I manage this business well?"

"Good decisions."

"That's helpful. Thank you. But, tell me, how do I learn to make good decisions, sir?"

"Experience."

"Yes, I see that. But one final thing, sir. How do I gain experience?"

"Bad decisions."

This is not, of course, to suggest in either business management or spiritual growth that one purposely makes mistakes. But inevitably mistakes can help us learn by experience—positive when possible, negative when necessary.

Someone said that there are three kinds of executives, those who know what will happen, those who make things happen, and those who don't know what happened!

The spiritually mature have had enough experience with the demands of righteousness that they know how to make the right things happen.

"Solid food is for the mature" (5:14). There is no better way to put it than this because "food" means a sound diet and "solid" is from the word that means "to stand." It is what we mean by "a square meal." It's what my father meant on cold Wisconsin mornings when he said oatmeal, simmered all night, would "stick to your ribs." Having grown somewhat on baby food, we are to take on some solids. When we have learned to swallow that, take that which is more hearty yet. We lose our taste for baby food and insist upon the solids of the Spirit.

Sermons in evangelistic meetings necessarily are elementary, the basic facts of the gospel. We should after that provide biblical messages in worship services for the spiritual growth of believers. As open and general as the congregations are likely to be, thought for the young Christians is important. But somewhere in the church's ministry, however, there must be a place for serious teaching of the deeper things of spiritual experience. There must be a ministry of the whole counsel of God as well as the initial story of salvation.

As I reviewed my goals in teaching freshman Bible, I realized that what I was teaching to high school graduates was little more than what they should have received from pastors, teachers, and parents back home. What I later taught to graduate students in theological seminary is what I should have been able to teach in Bible college.

I sit in Bible conference sessions during the day when the only people present have been pastors, missionaries, and lay officers for many years. But I keep hearing the same old messages preached by the same old preachers the same old way to the same old people. Milk! What's the solid food? Where are the mature?

I suggest we preach elementary sermons to the lost, sermons of substance to the young, and solid sermons to the growing.

If an individual is ahead of the congregation in readiness, let him take personal initiative to dig deeper by himself, for himself. If the sermons in his church are hopelessly shallow, let him supplement them with solid Bible teaching from any number of splendid radio broadcasts. And let him buy and study books and periodicals from evangelical publishers.

If local Bible conferences do not satisfy a hunger for solid food, let him enjoy the fellowship there and add to them those conferences that do.

The mature, who are nourished on solid food, also "work hard their perceptive senses." The word is used not only for such physical senses as hearing and seeing, but the ability to perceive. Mature people hear, but also think through the meaning of what they hear. More than seeing an object, they see into and through its nature.

Too many Christians are naive and gullible. The mature believer is perceptive and insightful. How so? Experience.

In walking through a San Antonio hotel lobby, a friend observed, "There are some runners."

With but a glance, I corrected, "Joggers. They haven't even gone out yet. How do I know? They're overdressed for the weather. They dress to keep warm while they jog. Real runners undress for freedom of movement, being warmed by the energy they generate."

Roll up your sleeves. Better yet, take your shirt off. That's the kind of exercise necessary—a hard workout—to train perceptive senses. This might be called spiritual aerobics. Runners don't avoid hills. They seek them. They run as hard as they are able so they are able for the hardest run. But many Christians jog through life on the flattest course they can find.

An unbelieving friend asks for an explanation of a moral decision I made. Do I evade the issue, claiming it to be private preference? Do I shield myself by pleading it to be against my religion? Or do I stick my neck out and attempt an answer?

The first time I am likely to get hit on the neck. I go home and ask myself some hard questions about what I said. I try new answers out on trusted brothers. Then I stick my neck out again.

I take risks. And I work hard my perceptive senses. To do what? To "discriminate between good and bad." The verb means "to judge between." Usually, it is between elements of the issue that often aren't as simple as assumed.

Wisdom sees subtle differences between objects where others are blinded by obvious similarities. And it is seeing subtle similarities when others see only differences.

Moral maturity is seeing good and seeing bad. It also sees the bad in the otherwise good and good in the otherwise bad. It recognizes when good is done for bad reasons and can separate good motives from bad acts.

The emotionally mature person—emotional maturity being essential for spiritual maturity—can be morally offended and intellectually differed with, without feelings being hurt. He can choose anger or happiness, as is appropriate to the occasion. And he can direct whatever the emotion to its correct object and control the intensity. He sustains as much stability as flexibility. His emotions are specific in application and comprehensive in resources.

By the same token, the spiritually mature person—building on the easier emotional maturity—can be morally offended and intellectually differed with, without hurting his spirit. He is not discouraged, much less demoralized. He does the right thing precisely because it is the right thing. He does it when there is no need or demand and without external reward.

This writer speaks in terms of maturity and dramatizes in pictures of entering into God's rest. He exhorts to go on to that maturity and to enter that rest. If we do not, he also warns, we will fall away.

WARNING: UNRESTORABLE FALLING *Hebrews 6:4-8*

The epistle's fourth warning is, "It is impossible for those" enlightened believers he describes "to be brought back to repentance" (6:4).

This statement is, for many, one of the most exasperating in the New Testament. It threatens theological explosion in several directions. As one begins to translate the language, it entangles him in a syntactical web that frustrates smooth English. Having gone through all that, this is how I think it comes out and what it amounts to.

Consider first the moral and spiritual condition described. It is carefully and fully stated, but not exaggerated or so much as labored. Six qualities are listed as already existing in such people. These believers are those who were enlightened; tasted the heavenly gift; became sharers of the Holy Spirit; tasted the good of the Word of God; tasted the powerful deeds of the coming age; and had fallen away.

If most versions had listed, rather than putting in the required sentence form, they would have included only the first five as qualities. The sixth "fallen away," would be stated separately as a distinct act. This is usually a result of a great effort to make theological sense and smooth reading. It is accomplished, however, only by a total reconstruction of the sentence structure and allowing the translation goal to override the language actually used. The meaning is sacrificed in favor of the expression.

The facts are that all six words have the same form, standing in coordination with each other, and that the author did not use the conditional *if*. He is not saying if a believer completes his enlightenment, tasting, and sharing and—after that—falls away, it is impossible to restore such a one. He says that a believer who sees enlightened, tastes clearly, shares meaningfully, and, at the same time, decides to fall away, that person will not be restored.

This person has been fully initiated into the Christian life. He chooses to fall away not despite what he knows, but on the basis of what he knows. He abuses his spiritual benefits to destroy what they made possible.

This is not, on the one hand, a person who is but tentatively introduced to the Christian life as a newborn or, on the other, already a mature believer acting consistently. The former has not yet reached this crisis, and the latter can reasonably, though not necessarily, be felt to have passed it.

It is crucial, I feel, to recognize the status of the person who is in danger. A sensitive, fresh Christian need not worry about ever being in such a critical state. Our Lord bears with his children who are inexperienced but learning.

However, a long-time Christian dare not relax under the assumption he is safe. The Lord will not indulge those who misuse their knowledge.

A mature and still maturing Christian moves confidently as a result of encouraging experiences with promises kept, although never presumptuously or carelessly. The enlightened believer doesn't know everything, but he knows enough to learn the balance of what he needs to know.

The subject has actually tasted those gifts beyond that which is common to all people on earth. He has tasted not only the good that comes now from the Word of God but also those things that will be fully functioning in the coming age.

"Sharing in" (NIV), or "partaking of" (KJV; RSV), the Holy Spirit has the same significance. Not yet having harvested the fruit of the Spirit, the person knows full well what that fruit is. The believer who falls away, having shared in the Spirit, does not ignore his fruit but rejects it.

Some Bible teachers are anxious to make this passage an attempt to defend God's fairness and reasonableness. In doing so, they cloud man's guilt and irrationality. Too many Christians have reacted, "Well, of course, if things should ever get that bad . . . "

Throughout his epistle, the writer addressed ordinary Christians. They are not hopeless cases, but people who need a better grip on their hopes because they are threatened by danger.

It helps to look at the nature of the falling that is of such concern. Although some translate it "commit apostasy" or "fall away," it is not the word *to apostatize,* often used by Paul. The word used here means literally "to fall beside." It was the word already used to describe those Hebrews whose bodies *fell* in the wilderness (3:17) and to warn that his readers should not *fall* after their example (4:11). He was writing here about people who fall by the wayside. They have had a good start on their spiritual journey, and they know clearly their destination, but they drop along the way, never reaching their goal.

The earlier Hebrews left Egypt dramatically. They felt keenly the weight of the Law laid on them at Sinai. They had a clear view of the gateway at Kadesh-Barnea. Enlightened by the Law and having tasted the miraculous power of God, the Hebrews turned around and wandered back into the wilderness. They dropped by the wayside.

The readers were also enlightened and had tasted, but they had additionally shared in the Holy Spirit. They now were in danger of dropping by the wayside of their spiritual journey from new birth to God's rest. The modern idiom "drop-out" comes easily to mind. Yet, that term better fits a relatively helpless, inexperienced person. We are talking about people who make a knowing choice, fully initiated quitters, those who should by now be nourished on solid food, but who have chosen to subsist on milk.

This description seems to indicate three possibilities:

1. A person can be tentatively introduced to the Christian life and fall down as a result of weakness or accident. That is correctable.
2. One can be fully initiated and never fall, resulting from strength and commitment. That is correct.
3. The Christian can be fully initiated and fall away as a result of rebellion and choice. That is incorrigible.

What is impossible, by definition, is that the incorrigible should ever be corrected. Of course, that's what the terms mean. This warning is altogether reasonable and not at all shocking. It can be no other way.

The impossibility, then, belongs not to God, his salvation, or reconciling by others, but to the case. Not a matter of God's ability, it is a question of the sinner's willingness.

Yet, some try to press the meaning of "impossible," hoping to squeeze from it some mitigation. Against this attempt, the writer asserts four things to be impossible, that "the blood of bulls and goats should take away sins" (10:4), "without faith it is impossible to please him" (11:6), "God should prove false" (6:18), and this.

If a Christian sins in full knowledge of the facts, not ignorant of them or not having kept known facts in mind, he will choose also not to repent. The decision to persist unrepentant is part of the decision to commit the sin. It isn't really that the person refuses to repent, since he has made a positive choice to sin and repentance is outside his frame of reference. Far from being an option, it is not even a possibility. It never comes to mind because the mind is set different.

This one knows the fact of the conditions necessary in order to accomplish the sin. These are his values. He knows the facts of the intended consequences of having committed the sin. These are his goals.

This sinner uses the knowledge of the conditions as his tool. He uses his knowledge of the consequences as his guide. Having done so, he has accomplished his purpose and is not about to surrender what he has thus achieved.

A foreign enemy that has declared war destroys defense emplacements of a nation it is about to invade. The nation attacked does not find it strange that the aggressor fails to repent. The offender has taken a logical step in a consciously and consistently evil movement.

The person who sins as the writer describes the act is behaving consistently and according to logic. What should surprise us is not the impossibility of his ever repenting. If anything should surprise us, it would be that he should as much as regret for a moment.

This, then, is the meaning of the choice to fall away knowingly. So to sin is not to risk failure to repent. It is the determination that such should never repent.

What about this act of restoration, stated as being impossible in this case? Used only here in the New Testament, the word "restore" or "brought back" isn't normally applied anywhere to an organism. It really has the force of a renovation, and repeated renovation eventually destroys the object. One can renovate a building by removing broken fixtures and replacing with new devices. After every original fixture has been replaced, the original building is simply gone and the word no longer applies.

Adding "again" to "renew" suggests the need for a continual renovation. The statement is clear enough. It is impossible to restore to repentance. This, in turn, is another way of saying that a person who has made up his mind doesn't choose to change his mind.

If you begin a thing without thinking it through, you can yet have second thoughts and complete your thinking by changing your mind, which was never made up. But there are no second thoughts to forethought. When you have thought the matter through before you start and choose a course, everything is settled before you start. There is nothing left to think about.

That's just how it is. It is impossible for a believer, who is at once fully initiated and fallen away, to be renewed into an attitude that would allow him to choose repentance from something to which he has already committed himself.

The author's explanation for this spiritual and psychological phenomenon is curious, and its full significance is not altogether clear. It is, in fact, so grotesque no simple statement will express it.

Such people, he said, "Crucify the Son of God on their own account and hold him up to public disgrace." The specific language taken literally seems to charge something utterly atrocious.

"They" is the subject that itself performs the action of "crucify again." They do so "to themselves." It is their own act of crucifying. Just as the Roman officials and Jewish leaders placed Jesus on a cross, some suggest at a busy crossroads near Jerusalem, such people are "subjecting him to public disgrace."

Purposeful falling away by the fully initiated, then, is not so much a rejection of the adequacy of Christ's sacrifice for them as it is a total rejection of Christ's person for any purpose. No longer accepted as Savior from chosen sin, he cannot be Lord of an ongoing life.

The fourth warning seems confining enough until the author slams the door to any escape with a shocking analogy. There being only two kinds of agricultural land, one must choose between them.

The land that receives a blessing from God is that which "drinks in the rain often falling on it and produces a crop useful to those for whom it was farmed" (6:7).

The other kind is, be warned: "But land that produces thorns and thistles is worthless and is in danger of being cursed. In the end it will be burned" (6:8).

Once again he used words that could cause fear. "To be burned" sounds frightfully like hell fire, though he didn't really say that.

This is the same point made by Jesus concerning a worthless vine, which is burned (John 15). That is what happens to fruitless vines and cropless fields. They cannot be used and, therefore, are unused. The only thing left to do is to dispose of them otherwise.

People are different in terms of the means of disposal, but not the fact. A useless Christian is unused. A Christian who exists without growth or produce suffers the agony fallow land is incapable of feeling. Better to be fallow land or barren vine that is burned than to be a fallow and barren Christian who rots everyday in his nothingness.

Most of us have been enlightened, have partaken of the Spirit, and have tasted the heavenly gift as well as the goodness of God's Word and the powers of the age to come. If we are not also falling by the wayside, it is still *today*. Being *today*, there is time in which to do something. Being fully initiated, there are things to do.

Yet, a peculiar danger confronts us. During our initiation into the full Christian life, we learn all the rules of living that life. Sometimes the rules are presented to us in a way that misses the point. We hear more about the letter of the law than its spirit. We get the impression that it is more important to escape through loopholes than to observe rules. Rather than using the rules as guides to growth, we abuse them as excuses from growth.

We are unable to mature without being enlightened about the Christian life. But an enlightened Christian can use what he has learned to avoid maturity at least as easily as he can to acquire it. We take well the warning about falling away if we recognize this liability and commit ourselves to constructive and productive use of what we have learned.

I was reared in a spiritually fertile environment of home and church. My parents and other elders gave me a rich heritage and made heavy investments in me. For some years, though, I exploited that favor and squandered the investment. I learned symbolic acts that put on a good show. The right words, even tone of voice and facial expression for embellishment, sounded pious. Looking around, I recognized most of my peers were doing the same. Every Christian needs to ask himself some hard questions about his language and behavior. As we measure ourselves, we need to discount appearance and count realities.

It isn't enough for a young person, for instance, to content himself with not having committed adultery. Did he kiss his girlfriend as an expression of affection or for sensual pleasure? Is it judged looseness when with a loose girl from school but all right when "fellowshipping" with a Christian girl?

Did the Christian lady use her knowledge of the Bible to help a sister gain spiritual growth or to defeat her in a theological squabble?

Do I recall just when the Holy Spirit actually spoke to me about doing something, or do I just claim he did to intimidate any opposition to my plans?

Another specific way to preclude the danger of the fully initiated is to become spiritual leaders of those to be initiated into the next level of Christian experience.

There is, in fact, a unique leadership contribution by first line leaders that simply cannot be made by leaders at the top. Witness, for instance, the proved experience at West Point. Certain leadership functions are exercised over the plebes by upperclassmen because it was found generations ago to be more effective than that of recently graduated second lieutenants or even (especially, in fact) field grade officers.

You use the little you have learned well when you teach it to a younger Christian who hasn't learned anything at all. And you learn so much, you thank the younger for what he has occasioned your having learned.

As an adequately initiated Christian, you may have more credibility and, therefore, effectiveness with the young Christian than do the deeply mature. The confident stride of the strong is often beyond comprehension by the weak child. Stumbling may make you self-conscious, but staying on your feet may be more believable and useable to that young one.

Once we have been spiritually enlightened, let's do at least these things. Let's insure we use our knowledge to continue learning. Let's use what we know to teach others who still need to learn it.

With this commitment, we'll not fall away. When we stumble in sin, we'll find it fully natural to repent and recover.

EXHORTATION: ENCOURAGEMENT FROM THE PAST
Hebrews 6:1, 2, 9-20

One of the more distinctive characteristics of exhortation is its breadth and clarity. The encouragement that is most effective remembers the past and sees into the future. It makes a connection between them. If a good thing has been done in the past, it can be done again in the future. And the present connects them.

The writer of Hebrews remembered the good things from his readers' past and forced them to recall those things. He had a view of their future and challenged them to reach it. He celebrated what they had done, although they chose to forget. He had more confidence in them than they did in themselves. They were ready to settle for being has-beens, but he would not allow it.

The courage they needed was to be found in at least three factors the writer explained: "You have a good beginning" (vv. 9-12). "You have helpful examples" (vv. 12-18). "You have hope in Christ" (vv. 19, 20).

"We really can go on from where we are now," the author exhorted. "Therefore, let us leave" those things that are peculiar to the first steps in the Christian walk "and go on to maturity" (6:1, 2). Let's step out and stride right until we arrive at our goal.

The writer listed a number of items quite necessary to being grounded in the new Christian life. These include "the elementary teachings about Christ," "the foundation of repentance," and "instruction about baptisms," probably catechetical type instruction in preparation for the public profession of faith.

It is easier for us to think of those particular things that were required in getting our feet on the ground in the kingdom of God. Now, he says, it is time to move on.

Keep those elementary things firmly in mind, but give immediate attention to the higher-level things yet to be learned. Continue to practice the first skills, but concentrate on greater skills. In such constructive affirmation we celebrate what is now in order to construct confidently what will become. It accepts whatever good now is present and builds upon it. Not to worry about how small the beginning, but to affirm the beginning.

I am still learning the value of constructive affirmation. I was reared in a culture where pride was considered to be necessarily and totally sinful, with no other consideration. We attacked pride, even at the cost of honesty. We recognized no difference between self-serving arrogance and honest gratitude for what God enabled us to accomplish.

Every accomplishment was put down lest one "let it go to his head." When complimented, we were to say "Oh, it's nothing. God did it." And we never caught the contradiction in our own platitude.

My early education was inhibited because it was motivated by the fear of remaining ignorant rather than the joy of becoming informed. It was oriented on the teacher's knowledge and my ability to secure her approval rather than my need for knowledge and the ability to earn self-approval.

My education took a marvelous turn when my eighth grade teacher affirmed what she saw in me and exhorted me to reach for what was possible.

I don't know why I didn't understand this in my early days of teaching. I remember most grievously my first attempts at teaching college students. The tests I put together were designed to uncover what the students did not know. Perhaps I thought this would embarrass them into learning, but it didn't. Perhaps I really wanted to show to them how much I knew, which also wasn't all that much.

When I became concerned about student needs more than professor power, I reoriented my teaching and testing. I learned—from my students—that they learn better by being rewarded for what they have learned than punished for what they haven't. They needed not embarrassment, but encouragement. Embarrassment demoralizes; encouragement motivates.

We need to present the gospel with this recognition. Too often do we humiliate people because of their sin rather than love them with Christ's compassion. We demoralize sinners when we should excite them about being born again. That only reinforces presumptions and erects barriers against conviction.

After his stern description of that purposeful falling by the wayside, the writer changed keys: "Though we speak thus, yet in your case, beloved, we feel sure of better things that belong to salvation" (v. 9, RSV).

His description is so terrible, it must have been reassuringly sweet to be addressed as "beloved." You're different from these, he asserted. And there's a whole lot more that belongs to your salvation than you have now. His burden, once again, was not that they should receive salvation. This they had, and they had it certainly.

But they didn't have all of their salvation, and they must not rest until they did. There were still ahead sins from which to recover and sins to avoid. Whichever, it is the salvation still needed.

But more than the saving from sin is the saving for righteousness. The past samples of righteousness stand out, and "God is not so unjust as to overlook" these things (v. 10, RSV).

Quite the contrary. Precisely because of them he expected more. God does not demand an unheard of impossibility. He expects an already demonstrated possibility. "We want each of you to show this same diligence to the very end, in order to make your hope sure" (v. 11).

Speaking for God, the writer said, "I am not really asking for something new from you. All I ask is that you do again what you have done before. The only new element in this exhortation is not to be sluggish about it."

But sluggish is exactly what they have been. Sluggish Christians. Never was a more accurate diagnosis of spiritual condition issued. No wonder. The writer had already observed their sluggishness in hearing (5:11). Sluggish learning results in sluggish performance. Sluggishness, whether in hearing or action, receiving or giving, directly opposes the need for diligence or earnestness to reach the full assurance of hope (6:11).

The word suggests industry and enterprise, not serendipity.

Is faith the passive resignation of an elderly saint who no longer fusses about anything? That may be the stereotype of a religious devotional in the Sunday supplement to the newspaper. Not in Hebrews. Its contribution would more likely be the exciting narrative of a middle-aged workman with sleeves rolled up and jaw set toward the completion of the job.

It is popular to picture faith as the quiet ease of one born with a delicate temperament, willing to accept whatever may come his way. It is biblical to recognize faith as the disturbing work of one who has developed a robust disposition, determined to achieve everything promised to him.

The writer encouraged, "Imitate those who through faith and patience inherit what has been promised" (v. 12). Discouragement that is sown by misunderstanding crops up here, too. We feel it is a mistake not to discriminate between pride in self and pride in Christ-in-us. It hits us, too, when we are told "take your eyes off men" and "Turn your eyes upon Jesus."

This, too, lacks discrimination. True enough, we must not copy the sinful or evil acts of anyone, saint or sinner. But how do I turn my eyes upon Jesus when his body isn't here to turn toward and there is no face to see?

Where else, and where better, can I find the face of Jesus than shining through the face of an earthly saint in whom he dwells by the power of the Spirit, as the hope of glory, so that this believer is conformed to the image of God's Son? I find Jesus most surely and most clearly and most helpfully in the lives of those in whom he lives his life. I find him more clearly still when several of those lives are congregated into the Body of Christ.

When the writer exhorted his readers to become imitators of more mature believers, he wasn't being blasphemous, but honest. This is helpful encouragement, not academic information.

It is true that I learned what kind of a father to become through study of the nature of the fatherhood of God. But, to be frank, I learned what the heavenly Father is like by my experience with my earthly father. Dad not only led me to Christ, I found Jesus Christ leading Dad.

When I first opened my eyes, it was Dad I saw and I kept my eyes on him. I liked what I saw, and I kept looking. As my focus became sharper, I saw Jesus in Dad. That's where I met Jesus. As I understood better what I saw, I realized what I liked most in Dad was Christ. In Mom, too, and in the spiritual uncles and aunts who surrounded me—they constituted the Body of Christ in our place.

I have since learned more about the theology of Christ than they ever knew. But for the reality of Christ, I am indebted to them. I still see Jesus in my memory of them, and I am still learning from them.

But we must choose human focus with care. It is those who have in fact received the promises who become the objects to be imitated or emulated.

The writer's word was that from which the English *mimic, mime,* and even *mimeograph* have come. These demonstrate the closeness of copy, but connote something mechanical that is foreign to the spiritual life.

If we understand the technical difference between the words, we can say the spiritual procedure is a duplication but not a replication. God, as he promised, was with Joshua as he was with Moses, a duplication of spiritual experience colored by strong distinctives for each.

This is what discipleship is all about. Ultimately, our discipleship is to the Lord himself, of course. But the term itself is used when such is experienced through a close interpersonal relationship that builds loyalty and then transfers it upward.

It is important to remember that John the Baptist said, "He must increase, but I must decrease." But, before that, it is also important to remember John called disciples to himself so that he could refer them to Jesus.

And, as a matter of history, the language has it that the Twelve and the larger number were disciples of Jesus more specifically than disciples of the Christ.

Study also the relationships of Moses and Joshua, Elijah and Elisha, Barnabas and Paul, Barnabas and John Mark, Paul and Timothy. The younger servants followed the older masters closely, and they emulated in their own lives the spiritual qualities found in the men who disciplined them.

As I was graduating from seminary, I searched for a spiritually mature man who was also an effective pastor. I knew I could learn from such a master pastor things no professor could teach. I could find in him what I could find in no book. Sadly, no such pastor was available. Some of the mistakes I made subsequently would have been unnecessary if I had been at the side of such a man. I still need a Paul to whom I can be a Timothy, even though there are younger men who have asked me to be their Paul.

We all need such people, and we should all search until we find one. I don't refer just to professional or ministerial skills. More important are spiritual and moral mentors.

I do not have a pastor specifically in mind. We enable our own care by being close, open, and honest with our pastors. Not only must we not hide from him any spiritual fact in our lives, we should insure he knows us well, thoroughly and accurately. We must confess the worst as well as display the best.

An elder brother or sister in the Lord is my suggestion, one who is free from pastoral predispositions. Each of us should have one who can relate to us privately and individually. We need someone who can almost indulge us without political or institutional worry about being fair with others.

In your church may be an individual who has never exercised any public leadership and isn't popularly known as a spiritual giant. You may discover in that person the one whom God has specially prepared to be your particular spiritual guide. In fact, that individual may never have perceived himself in any such role. But he has the strength and richness uniquely appropriate for your weakness and blandness. Discover each other.

How? Classified ads and pulpit announcements won't do it. I suggest we simply get to know each other as individuals rather than merely fellow church members. Then pray that the Holy Spirit will identify one of these relationships as that special one which is needed.

We require the spiritual leadership of pastors and elder brothers and sisters. And we need the spiritual fellowship of our peers. I think it is as important to find a special friend who is about where we are spiritually and to create a covenant of mutual support and encouragement.

There is usually some brother or sister who needs you as an elder. It may be only days that separate your respective new births, and only inches may be counted between your stages of growth. But it is likely to be enough for you to gain through giving. We do well to create and move about in a spiritual network.

The goal toward which we move is inheriting the promises. The way we move is through "faith and persistence." If "faith" sounds passive to some, "persistence" cannot. And "persistence" is a necessary rendering of the writer's word because "patience" still sounds too passive. The word used contains the element of large amounts of laboring.

Patience is sitting by passively while something happens to us. Persistence is making sure we make the right thing happen. A spectator sits by patiently while a runner presses on and goes on with persistence. The persistence that moves us toward inheriting the promises is an expression of the faith. Faith is not a passive possession. It is an active practice.

Take Abraham. He was such a person who can be emulated. The writer of Hebrews put Abraham forward as an example for good reasons. Specifically, in relation to his readers, Abraham was among those from whom he chose. To the Jewish mind, or any that respected Jewish values, Abraham was the preeminent illustration of a man of active faith. He did not have faith by sitting patiently in Ur. He exercised faith by getting up and going.

Abraham, as all people of faith, acted purposefully without necessarily understanding the purpose. He moved with a sense of direction without seeing the direction. He was a man of destiny without reaching his destination. As Paul put it about the patriarch, "in hope he believed against hope" (Rom. 4:18, RSV). The writer of Hebrews stated, "And so after waiting patiently, Abraham received what was promised" (v. 15).

Did he, now? God promised him a people and a land. Although he was surprised by the birth of Isaac, he never lived to see the tribes of the sons of Israel. Yet, he was the happy "Father of the Many." He arrived on the land promised, but the promised land was never given to him. He was a stranger on the land in which he was promised to be sovereign. He was promised the land on which he stood, but that land was never constituted the land of promise while he stood on it. No matter. The promise was given, and he acted the faith that made it a reality. Abraham experienced the promise without possessing it.

Abraham is the prime example of a believer who ended well and, so, could experience beyond the end. Abraham's body occupied space, but his spirit soared infinitely. His days were numbered, but he lives eternally. He experienced more than he possessed. Faith is that way. It can be so for us.

Faith that is held as a possession does not produce and is a profitless possession. Faith that is acted upon produces an experience beyond what could ever be possessed within time and space.

Strange. Standing atop a hill in Canaan and surveying the landscape stretched in all directions beyond him, Abraham was viewing the land promised to him. He was literally standing upon the promised land. Although he had arrived geographically, the geography was not his. He was at the destination, but he hadn't reached his destiny.

He had to purchase land. He was tolerated by the natives as a foreign alien journeying there just so long. Abraham was a visitor to a land of which he was promised to become lord. Economic necessity forced him to desert even this. He returned only to be buried. No matter. He experienced both the land and the people promised just as if he possessed and saw them. Not only was his faith active, it was real. Abraham learned that the experience of faith brings stronger confidence and richer joy than the illusion of physical possessions.

In fact, mere possession can deceive us into thinking we have something of significance. Possession may be actual, but it isn't real until we experience the purpose of the thing possessed.

The thousands who have been conned into purchase of Florida lots have learned they possess land without value. People of spirit with a sensitivity to God's created nature, on the other hand, enjoy their visits to lovely public spots in the same state and experience them as many landlords never have. There's something more real than possession.

Also strange is the fact that Abraham experienced something he never possessed. Many of us, in regard to salvation, fail to experience something we already possess.

How do we follow Abraham's example? How about the Kingdom of God? Are we any more strangers on this earth than Abraham was in Canaan? The Creator promised this earth to his children for whom he made it. It is ours. We belong here. Earth is our home.

We are indeed strangers to this present evil social system resulting from sin and a corruption of God's creation. But we, nevertheless, stand on an earth belonging to our Lord and promised to us.

We may not be able to possess the land as the Kingdom of God, but we can, and must, experience the Kingdom of God within the world. This may be enemy-occupied territory, but we are loyal citizens of the Kingdom and royal children of the King. As we persist in living obediently and loyally under the absolute reign of God as our one Sovereign, we obtain the Kingdom promised.

It remains for Christ to return to earth himself to establish his Kingdom politically and to occupy the earth physically. But through active faith and determined persistence, we can obtain now what the unfaithful and sluggish can only see later.

We may be strangers within worldly society, but we are native citizens of the earth and its community of faith. The real strangers on earth are those who do not know its King as their personal Lord and Savior. And for those who have formally accepted him as Savior but not submitted to him also as Lord, they live strangely in an unfamiliar community.

No matter that the world is evil. Just don't fall back into it. Go on. Experience what God has promised, and act as if we possess the world in which we practice our faith.

When we respond to God's revealed will, we will do what God wants despite the decisions of men. When hindrances are erected before us, let us move through them as if they didn't exist because, for the one who moves us, they don't.

If we go on, we can experience all that God has promised. The person of faith is the one who emulates Abraham and, through faith and persistence, obtains the promises.

Having been reassured by our own early successes and challenged by the greater achievements of those we emulate, let's be finally convinced by the hope Jesus Christ has established for us.

After substantial reasoning about the oath by which God pledged his promise to Abraham (vv.13-16), the writer made the application to the present day:

> Because God wanted to make the unchanging nature of his purpose very clear to the heirs of what was promised, he confirmed it with an oath. God did this so that, by two unchangeable things in which it is impossible for God to lie, we who have fled to take hold of the hope offered to us may be greatly encouraged (vv. 17, 18).

There it is. Better than the success in our past we had almost forgotten. Better, even, than the victories of others we hadn't thought we could reach.

We can have "strong encouragement to secure the hope set before us."

The hope set before us?:

> We have this as an anchor for the soul, firm and secure. It enters the inner sanctuary behind the curtain, where Jesus, who went before us, has entered on our behalf (vv. 19, 20).

The picture the writer created is, of course, the tabernacle with its three compartments. The "inner place" is the Holy of

Holies, entered only on the annual Day of Atonement. In several portions of the epistle, at which we are not looking this time through, we find the ultimate sanctuary of the new covenant to be heaven and the innermost room to be the throne of God where Christ sits on the right hand to intercede for us.

When the resurrected Jesus ascended from earth and returned bodily to the Father in heaven, he acted as a forerunner (one who runs the required course before the main body runs it) on our behalf. He is like a foot runner who hurries ahead of the diplomat to announce his approach and present his request.

The forerunner does what only he can do and he does it so the rest do not need to attempt those things but can give their attention to what they must for themselves.

An anchor is affixed to bedrock so that the ship cannot drift. A diver has gone down from the ship to the bottom of the sea and anchors it to something that cannot be moved. He stays there to insure its security. Those on board do not see the anchor, but they saw the diver carry it down and they see the taut line holding their ship stable.

The worshippers saw a Melchizedek priest enter into the innermost altar with his own blood in place of theirs. No need for the uneasiness of waiting for the next annual day because this priest stays with the sacrifice, offering it constantly.

The world's most competent mountain climber preceeded the main body of the climbing party and reached the summit. There he affixed a fastening device to the outcropping of the mountain's bedrock. A nylon rope extends from that fix down the mountainside to its base. We begin to climb, persistently pulling ourselves up the rope laid in place for us.

We are halfway up the mountain and becoming frightened. We've done well so far, and those we follow have gone the distance. Clouds obscure the view at the top, and we can't see the end and its security. But we see the rope, and we grip it tightly because we know where it leads and who put it in place.

It's dangerous where we are. But the greatest danger in where we are is staying where we are. If we freeze, our arms will tire and we'll lose our grip. If we hold the rope sluggishly, it'll slip from hand. We'll fall back.

As dangerous as it undeniably is, the only safe course is to keep climbing to wherever the rope leads. We know who put it in place, and we know he has secured it where he is. We gain strong encouragement, and grip the rope firmly.

We go on persistently. We remember the past, but we don't look down. We can't see the top, but we keep looking up.

FIVE

DRAW NEAR, LEST YOU WALK AWAY
HEBREWS 10:19-39

The campus queen announced an open house. She was one of those statuesque beauties with a charming personality; fellows had always crowded around and followed whenever they could. Even women students enjoyed being with her since she was genuinely nice and a good friend to all who knew her.

Not everyone, of course, had had the good fortune to meet her. Many fellows admired from a distance and fantasized her floating into their lives. The promised opportunity arrived by notices posted on bulletin boards around campus—an open house. Though the invitation was issued in the names of all girls who roomed there, everyone understood it to be an incredibly gracious offer by the one whom all wanted to meet. At least, such is the only thing that came to most of their minds.

One freshman was especially agog about the lady. His heart had leaped at the notice. After grooming as never before, he dressed in his best clothing. Strange how fast the blood can flow when the breath comes so hard. Now he lingers across the street, leaning against a tree. He had arrived, but he fears to cross and approach the house. This is too good to be true, and he knows he hasn't a chance with her. Yet, there was the invitation and here is the party.

As they pass him on the way to the house, several students greet him and say something about going in. A sensitive one even comes back before entering and specifically encourages this timorous one. Don't be afraid; you're welcome.

It's a little obvious. Several times he starts to cross, but turns back.

Though the cocky fellows ridicule, the hostess has compassion. Will one of the other girls wave him on in? When one goes onto the porch to do so, he quickly turns away as if looking elsewhere. A second tries her luck and even calls to him, "Come on in." But he pretends not to hear.

Go on over, and invite the silly boy in. He's making me nervous now.

So one of the fellows complies. Excuses. No end to them. He happens just to be passing by. He isn't sure he has the time. He doesn't really know anyone there.

Without having joined the party, the reluctant freshman has made himself the center of attention. Finally, in disgust, one of the several fellows stalks over and says, "Look, either join the party or get out of the neighborhood. You can either come in, or you can walk away. But you can't just keep standing here. When she invited everyone, that meant you, too. You're welcome to come in and join the fun. But you can't mope outside and spoil the fun inside. We won't put up with this nonsense."

He never wanted to come to the party, anyway. He just came by to see who is there. And as he thought, it is no one but the big shots who had never had any time for him before. Besides, she doesn't really mean the invitation, but only wants to make fun of him.

Come to think about it, he is pretty mad about the whole thing. There is no way he is going to stick his neck out and walk into that kind of circus.

He walks away.

What this young man did is very much what some believers do. Walk away. From what? The historic reference in the Epistle to the Hebrews is not to the nation Israel, at Kadesh-Barnea, rebelliously refusing to enter the land of promise. Rather, the author is exhorting his readers to something even the ancient Hebrews could not then have done. The writer was talking about one of those better things open to us through the new covenant in Jesus Christ, which was closed to Israel under the old covenant.

The Christian can draw near to God the Father, without a priest. We can become intimate with the Holy God, close to the Almighty.

As always, when God offers mankind a precious, sacred thing, this offer cannot forever be ignored. God's offers are never "take it or leave it." They are always "take it or it will be taken from you."

If we do not lay hold, we will drift away. If we do not do it, we will disbelieve. If we do not go on, we will fall back. No surprises, then. If we do not draw near, we will walk away.

Drawing near to God, becoming intimate with God, is a choice or a rejection. When Israel refused to enter the land, the people did not stand forever at Kadesh-Barnea, looking at the promise. The people chose to walk away from the land, and they never got near it again.

So, too, with the offer of drawing near to God in immediate worship and intimate fellowship. If we draw near, we can go on to full salvation. We can experience salvation, the saving life, in every sense, and we can experience every aspect of salvation.

The epistle's fourth exhortation is to draw near, to become intimate with God. The fifth and final warning is that there is no provision for deliberate and knowledgeable sin. Christ's sacrifice was not made to provide salvation from that kind of sinning.

The text for this chapter begins the practical section of the epistle. From Hebrews 1:1 to 10:18, the writer was primarily concerned to lay a foundation of doctrinal concepts. Although he continually inserted specific behaviors to illustrate the doctrines' practice, it is at this point the practice of the faith comes to the forefront. The doctrinal explanations are, from here on, background to the behavior encouraged.

This fifth warning, about deliberate and knowledgeable sin, completes the writer's teaching concerning the negative aspect of salvation, the consequence of failing to use salvation.

The fifth exhortation, in essence was, "Choose to become intimate with God or you will walk away when you could have gone on to full salvation."

DRAWING NEAR, vv. 19-25

Let's confidently draw near to God in fellowship so we live in his holiness. It was no light or casual thing for the writer to encourage his readers in this way. The teaching collided with the priests' restrictions, since the Law required the people to stand at a distance from the act of sacrifice. The people were to rely on those intermediaries to perform worship services on their behalf. Even the prophets, who had condemned Israel's mechanical observance of the Law and challenged the people to practical morality, could not have gone so far.

The writer's challenge took Christ's fulfillment of the Law in the offering of "the blood of Jesus" (v. 19) as the ultimate sacrifice, which established a new covenant (testament), "the new and living way" (v. 20).

Before the veil that separated the holiest from the holy place was torn at the time of the crucifixion, separation was stressed and distance was enforced. The people brought their animals to the door of the outer court and surrendered them to a priest, who alone could take the offerings inside. The people then withdrew to safety. The Levites were restrained within the court while only the priests fearfully ventured into the holy place. Even they went no farther into the tabernacle. Only the high priest dared enter the holiest, and then only on the annual Day of Atonement. While he was doing this, the people quite literally held their breath until he returned safely. To stand before the Glory of God resting over the Ark of the Covenant was a fearful thing.

But Christ had done all this once for all, for all people, for all time. The readers of this epistle were then, as we are now, under a new covenant. The great separation of righteousness from sin had been shown by the Law. The differences between the holy and the profane had been dramatized. To stand at a distance from the sacrifice was no longer necessary, and standing at a distance from God is both unacceptable and harmful.

Standing formally at a distance from God while a priest performs a ceremony, in contrast to personally drawing near to God in fellowship, shows the difference betweens religion and spirituality.

Religion is an institutionalized system of forms and ceremonies only symbolic of spiritual realities. Spirituality is personal experience, living what is spiritually real.

God gave a religion to Israel, and the Hebrews practiced it. He revealed this religion progressively through his promise to Abraham, the Law through Moses, and the preaching of the prophets. It was a good religion, and it did the best any intensive religion can.

But that was never considered to be good enough, and there were better things promised. These came through God's Son, and the Christ is the fulfillment of the Law. He accomplished what the Law could only describe. He gives what the Law could never promise.

The dynamic fulfillment of the Law in the person of God's Son lightened the oppressive burden of religion and frees us for the joy of spiritual experience. Without the intervention of a priest, we now have direct access to God.

This "new and living way" is that which Christ "opened for us through the curtain, that is, through his flesh" because "we have a great priest over the house of God" (vv. 20-21, RSV).

Despite all this, these "Hebrews" of the new covenant stood at a distance from God as did those under the Law. It isn't that they were anxious to return to the tyranny of the Law or even so much that they were traditionally tied to Judaism. They just wanted to be more religious than spiritual.

There is a certain comfort and convenience to religion, which seems to excuse from the responsibilities and demands of spiritual living.

The letter of the Law always closes limitations beyond which one need never grow. This is comforting. The spirit opens opportunities that know nothing of limits. That's scary.

The writer exhorted, "Draw spiritually near God." He warned, "Don't walk away to a religious distance."

The same frightful thing happens to Christians today. Many of us never openly rebel against God and plunge into worldly sin. We privately pull back from experience and walk into religion. We don't turn worldly. We become religious.

Drawing near to God is a spiritual experience, an experience with reality rather than just an exercise of religion.

Religiosity is more an attitude than an activity. It is easy to assume that religion must be an organized ecclesiastical structure, formalized by a published liturgical manual, or recited in versified creed.

Make no mistake about it. We are all religious to some extent. We all need some religious starters and support. We need to remember that any religion can turn bad.

Religion itself is morally and spiritually neutral. True religion, well used, helps a spiritually weak believer draw near to God. Badly used, it prevents a person from drawing near. Religion is intended to convey a human to God. If it gets us there, it's good. If it doesn't, it is bad. However, bad religion more characteristically takes us further away from God. It is equally effective for that.

I want to be spiritual, not religious. I will use religious devices as much and as often as I need them in order to reach spiritual reality. As I experience spiritually, I intend to drop the devices as no longer useful.

The balance is to be as religious as is necessary to become regularly spiritual but to be religious no more—or religious no longer—than is necessary for this purpose. In a word, to be as religious as necessary but as spiritual as possible.

Let's not discard a help because it's religious. We may need the help to become spiritual.

How do I know I have gone beyond religion and have drawn near to God? More accurately, because of the nature of salvation and spiritual growth, how do I know I am in the state of continually drawing nearer to God?

First, I can feel it. Never was the subjective feeling clearer or more real for me than during basic training at Fort Riley, Kansas. For several weeks I had been increasingly oppressed with a sense of utter loneliness in an evil world. At the first opportunity to attend a chapel service, I prayed during the organ prelude. And I cried, "God is here, and I can feel him now. I belong here."

At that time of severe emotional and social pressure, I needed to draw closer to God and to regain spiritual strength and moral commitment. But I needed religion to get me there. And it did.

The device God chose to use that morning was the small silver cross in each lapel of the chaplain's uniform. In my nonliturgical background, women didn't hang crosses around their necks and men didn't put them in their lapels. Religious people did that. The spiritual carried red Scofield Bibles. But the chaplain wore crosses, and I fixed my eyes on them. "Jesus Christ is here, I thought. There is his cross."

I felt near to God.

I continued to feel near him when I left the chapel, when I returned to the barracks and—in the field—wherever I was.

Second, others see it. Within a week, I talked with Ralph for the first time. We hadn't chatted more than a few minutes before each sensed in each other the Lord that both of us were trying very hard to stay close to. It happened that the chaplain was Lutheran and Ralph was Christian Reformed.

When there is a personal closeness, others sense and understand it. Several times visitors to our church had identified Allison as my daughter when she was standing next to me. I recognized what they saw while I was the guest preacher in another church. I picked out the pastor's daughter, standing next to him. She stood in relation to him as only a daughter could, not quite touching, but with an intimate closeness that comes naturally when one belongs to the other.

Drawing near to God like that is intimate fellowship that seems an audacious suggestion.

I have wondered if it is worth the risks of the easy-come, easy-go attitude many today have toward God and sacred things. Services intended for worship are upset by casual behavior and confused by flippant chattering. Prayers lack a sense of awe. Then I recall the difference between intimacy and that kind of familiarity. Closeness to God in fellowship is not, I also recall, the same as social affront.

Those with an easy familiarity with God have not drawn near in worship. They seem to stand near him and slap him on the back. The epistle's picture has us sitting respectfully at the Lord's feet, looking up in awe and love.

Drawing near is "with a true heart in full assurance of faith, with our hearts sprinkled clean from an evil conscience and our bodies washed with pure water" (v. 22, RSV). That is to say, we will have sustained a moral change from a spiritual experience. While this is not religion as such, it is what religion is intended to lead to.

We know we have succeeded in drawing near to God when the nearness has changed us. We know that a religious worship service has been spiritually effective, for instance, because worshipers are different when they leave from what they were when they arrived.

Worship is the celebration of the worthship of God in and of himself. Although it begins with standing in awe before his absolute holiness, it grows into participation in that holiness so that we too become holy. The effectiveness of worship is proved by the demonstration of our holiness in the way we behave before people and the way we treat each other.

When we gather for worship, the goal is not to receive a feeling that pleases us. The goal is for us to offer worship that pleases God. The success of a worship service depends not on whether or not we are pleased with the service but whether or not God is pleased with us.

This much Israel always understood. In their most rebellious moments, we do not read anywhere in the Old Testament about Hebrews asking those questions which would have been the equivalent of those which are popular today. Did the high priest keep his staff in line? Were all the priests dressed modestly and inexpensively? Had the Levites sung that song before? Did they pay enough attention to the announcements? Did the service get out on time?

We know that something has happened, that we have been changed, when we sustain the confidence of nearness. The term "confidence" appears often in Hebrews and the concept is crucial to its exhortations. We must "hold fast the confidence" (3:6). "Let us approach the throne of grace with confidence" (4:16). Confidence "has a great reward" (10:35).

The Greek word is built from two words which mean "all" and "word." Literally, it means "all-word." English expresses the thought with several idioms. "When all is said and done and you are in full possession of all the facts," you are confident. It allows us to approach an otherwise difficult task with ease. The one who knew what to do "walked right on in as if he owned the place," we would say. The runner on the last leg of the course picks up the pace on hearing, "It's downhill from here on."

The English comes from two Latin words, *con* (the intensive "with") plus *fides* ("faith"). Confidence is acting "with-faith."

In Hebrews, at least, the word is not at all a subjective, emotional attitude. It stands strong with an objective, moral character. Confidence is sustained not because of a quantity within the mind of the person but a quality out there.

We have confidence to enter and we can draw near with full assurance because Christ has created for us "a new and living way" and then dedicated it to our use.

The exhortation to draw near produces additional encouragements. "Let us hold fast the confession of our hope without wavering" (v. 23) and "Let us consider how to stir up one another to love and good works" (v. 24).

We draw near to God confident of our acceptability in Christ, and we go on in life confidently accomplishing the results of confidence. The life of faith is the life of confidence. It knows what it is about, and it is about its business.

Along with the exhortation of drawing near to God and that of holding fast the confession of our hope comes, "Let us consider how we may spur one another on toward love and good deeds. Let us not give up meeting together . . . but let us encourage one another" (vv. 24, 25).

If drawing near to God results in a changed life, how else can we be certain that our lives have been changed? By our changing, in turn, the lives of others. If others have difficulty examining a change within our hearts, let them experience it in the change it inspires within their own hearts. The believers who are actually near God are those who are authentically near each other.

In some ways the King James Version's more awkward rendition comes closer to the writer's meaning than most modern versions. "Let us consider one another." The object of the verb "consider" is "one another." Our interest is not in methods, but people—not social manipulation so that we develop a skill and then find someone on whom to use it. Our interest is people and then what we can do to help them.

Let us be so considerate of our brothers' value and potential that we excite them to love and good works. Good parents are not those who merely love their children. Nor is it enough to make them merely lovely people. Truly successful parents love them so constructively that they create loving persons of their children.

When we have learned well to love and do good works, it is time we learn to be so considerate of others that we excite them to loving and doing good works.

I found it necessary to require my Bible college students to come to tests prepared with a pencil for test sheet marking. It was an arbitrary rule—no pencil, no test.

In one class of sixty students, just one girl failed to come with a pencil. I felt sorry for her, since it was an understandable failure.

One face lit up. A fellow broke his pencil into two pieces and began to hand one to his classmate. His face brightened more, and he took the broken piece to the sharpener to give her a pencil ready to use.

Although she had thanked him with obvious gratitude and although it had cheered all the others, I stopped her as she was leaving. "Are you going to let a good thing like this die? Can you think of a way to keep it going?"

As she entered the classroom for the next session, she held out to her friend a package of new pencils. She withdrew them and, smiling the more, took them to the sharpener and sharpened them all—to the delighted applause of the class.

At the next test, at least ten students held up extra pencils: "Pencil, anyone?" I follow some of these students and know that they are still doing things like that. The things are growing in significance and the good deeds in their results.

The fellowship of the Body of Christ is in "encouraging one another, and all the more as you see the Day drawing near" (v. 25, RSV).

The hallmark of a healthy congregation is not its profession to love one another, but in actually caring for each other and encouraging one another. Church is where we should be able to go to be encouraged by the Lord through our brothers and sisters.

Often believers have been discouraged from meeting together because they were chronically discouraged by others when they had attended public services. Sometimes Christians have neglected to meet together precisely because they do not wish to encourage others. Some of these stay home with the strange hope that they will be called on and get individual attention. One might think these understand the value of encouragement since they seek it. Yet they look not for encouragement, but pampering.

The place to go to encourage one another is the public assembly for worship of God and fellowship with our brothers. When we worship God, we experience fellowship with him.

Consider the service of communion. We begin by thinking about the death of Christ—the body that was broken and the blood that was shed for us. We rise from communion together, and together return to the world outside there to live a common testimony.

A Southern Baptist chaplain with whom I served at Fort Sheridan, Illinois, had become estranged from his teenaged son. They actually loved each other, but conflicts had almost destroyed the sense of that love. They longed for reconciliation, but neither knew how to go about it. I had talked with each, but had failed to bring them together.

When we held communion in the post chapel, we gave worshipers the option of remaining in the pew to be served there or coming to the rail to receive the elements. The father had come to the rail, but his son remained in the pew. I'm not sure if the son intended to participate in communion, but I noticed him studying his father kneeling at the rail. I think he knew his father was praying for him. I motioned for the next person to move over to create another space at the altar rail. As I looked to the boy to invite him down, I saw him coming forward confidently, though under great emotion. He knew he could draw near because a way had been opened for him. He was confident he would be accepted since he knew his father's love and that he was praying for him.

Each put one arm around the other's shoulder and used the other hand for the bread and wine. They communed with the Savior who had given each his love for the other. He is also the Lord who brought father and son back together as brothers in Christ.

WALKING AWAY Hebrews 10:26-31

If we choose not to draw near, we choose to walk away. Life's that way— always moving and changing. It refuses to stand still. If a living being does not move on, he will move aside or back or somewhere, but he will move.

The fifth and final warning is: "There is no provision for deliberate and knowledgeable sin." If you choose to persist in the sinning life, be advised that Christ's sacrifice is not intended for salvation from that sinning.

> If we deliberately keep on sinning after we have received the knowledge of the truth, no sacrifice for sins is left, but only a fearful expectation of judgment and of raging fire that will consume the enemies of God (vv. 26, 27).

This warning has the same sense as the others. We should also expect it to arrive with increased force. The warning is meant to disturb.

The two serious elements in both warnings are the seriousness of the sin and the reasonableness of judgment—the seriousness of consequence and the crisis for response.

The kind of sin mentioned here is as heavily qualified as we found for the previous warning about having been "enlightened . . . tasted the heavenly gift . . . became partakers . . . tasted the goodness . . ." (6:4, 5).

The qualifications here are also several. The verb for "sin" is in the durative form and carries the sense "persist in sinning." Not a one-time act or occasional indulgences, it describes an unrelieved continuity of sinning. Second, the sinning is deliberate or willful, not an accident of emotions. The sin is selected and the act chosen. This isn't describing a well-meaning, thoughtless person, who wanders carelessly into unacceptable territory. This person is a schemer who plans his trip carefully and resolutely executes his plan.

The sin is also knowledgeable. Both *knowledge* and *truth* are strengthened by the definite articles, *the* knowledge of *the* truth. We are talking about a learned doctor in the field.

It takes a Christian of some substance and experience to sin like this. But they are there. They know sin well enough to use it with maximum force. They know holiness well enough to know how it is most seriously offended.

Such people understand human perverseness sufficiently to be able to exploit it, and righteousness well enough to corrupt it.

I once read an autopsy report in which the medical examiner remarked, "This death had to be inflicted by someone who has a good knowledge of poisons and a thorough understanding of how the body ingests to be able to accomplish what he did." The report almost said, "It takes a physician to do a job like this."

The general public regularly finds it difficult to conceive heinous crimes as having been committed by normal people. Reading news reports of such, the immediate reaction tends to be, "He must be crazy. No sane person could ever do such a horrible thing." Juries, too, seem easily convinced that bizarre deeds could only be perpetrated by the insane.

The fact of the matter is, however, that the most despicable crimes are committed by people in full possession of their faculties and who know exactly what they are doing. No necessary relationship exists between the terribleness of a crime and mental incompetence. When a relationship does exist between such a crime and mental ability, it is more often one strong enough mentally for the crime.

The problem we have is our fear to admit normal people are capable of the worst crimes, since it is perceived as such a threat to our own sense of security. We fail to give enough respect to the power of sin and the human capacity to sin. Our consideration should not be only of that, since such power can come from Satan as well as from the Holy Spirit. Most of us are unprepared to understand the incredible power of Satan when he actually does his work within a human heart and mind.

"Satan is at work in our midst" is too flippantly and too frequently tossed around for us to take seriously the real work of Satan. This text describes the high quality work he accomplishes.

We award Satan far too much credit for the trouble we are in, and flatter ourselves outrageously with suggestions that we are worth Satan's attention. There are few Christians with whom Satan needs to bother. Most of us are quite capable in and of ourselves to keep things stirred up. Our assigning to Satan the responsibility for our sins is more often a cop-out from moral and spiritual accountability.

Satan's greatest targets are effective Christian servants. When he defeats one of them, it is a negative miracle. We are as awed by Satan's destructive miracles as God's constructive miracles.

When a Christian believer has once been enlightened, has tasted the heavenly gift as well as the goodness of the Word of

God and the powers of the age to come, has become a partaker of the Holy Spirit, has received the full knowledge of the truth, Satan is interested in him. If he can persuade this person to turn aside and deliberately persist in sinning, Satan has accomplished something completely worth his while.

This should be quite believable and not at all surprising. The Christian described here is no ordinary sinning person, but a prize possession of Satan. The hardest person to win back to fellowship with Christ is the one who had once known Christ the best and then had chosen to turn aside and had chosen to sin. Hard? Sometimes it is impossible.

What remains for him? Not restoration to repentance since he had already chosen not to repent. Not a sacrifice since none was ever offered for this.

If it is difficult to understand the deliberate sin described—and, surely, it is—I find it exceedingly difficult to understand how the writer of Hebrews could make the statement that he did about sacrifice when it necessarily reflects upon the only real sacrifice, that of Christ. Is this to say that the ultimate sacrifice of his own blood by God's eternal Son is incapable of saving some sinner? Could there be any sinner so vile he could not be saved by God's redemptive work in Christ? Could it ever be said that there could be any sin so gross that it could not be atoned for by Calvary?

These questions are understandable, and I ask them. But they are not good questions because to ask them is, once again, to go beyond what the Bible says.

The writer had already given full and sufficient attention to the greatness of Christ's sacrifice. The attention here is not on his sacrifice, but upon deliberate sinning by a fully knowledgeable person. The two just don't apply.

If a deliberate/knowledgeable/persistent sinner challenges the adequacy of Christ's sacrifice, the writer refused to discuss the matter. A totally different question is in front of us, and the two must not be mixed.

Such was the perspective I heard in a conference at Fitzsimons Army Medical Center in Denver. The subject of the conference was critical trauma sustained by hang-gliding youth on the nearby mountains. These kids would climb to the top of a cliff and jump into space, hoping to glide smoothly to a safe landing hundreds of feet below and, hopefully, miles distant. At least as often, they crashed into the side of a cliff. In addition to those regularly killed, scores suffered crushed bones, torn flesh, and mutilated internal organs.

One highly skilled and outstandingly successful surgeon complained, "These young kids purposely throw their healthy, strong bodies off a cliff and dare fate to kill them. They smash themselves up as no mugger could ever do and only the worst of auto accidents could."

Finally the surgeon said, " 'Good ol' Doc' is not here for that sort of thing. I'm here to heal sick people and save accident victims. My surgical skills are not for hire by arrogant exhibitionists or imbeciles obsessed with suicide. Don't bring them to me." Of course, he went back to work performing his "miracles" on the hang-glider accident patients, but he made his point, one I hope we can all see. Salvation from sin is seriously challenged by deliberate sin, just as deliberate risk on a hang glider seriously challenges the skills of medical resources.

The sacrifice offered by Christ is intended to give new spiritual life to spiritually dead people. That sacrifice does not prevent a spiritually alive believer from sinning, nor does it force him to repent of the sin he has chosen. That was never its purpose. And since Christ only offered one sacrifice, there no longer remains another sacrifice for sins when a person persists in deliberate sinning.

Christ's sacrifice is, to be sure, sufficient atonement to accomplish full salvation, but the sacrifice did not include deliberate, knowledgeable sinning from which there would be no repentance.

The author's teaching is conceptually deep, so that no theological formula is going to easily explain it.

The family was hiking on Mount Rainier in Washington state when we found the road blocked by a permanent barricade. It wasn't really blocked in every sense, because we could have walked around and continued toward an overlook that offered an unusual view. We were also confronted by a large sign: "DANGER DO NOT PASS BEYOND THIS POINT."

It was an impressive warning, one meant to be taken seriously. I confess, I don't always take every sign seriously, but this just couldn't be ignored.

It did stir curiosity, however. I never questioned the reason for the warning, but I wondered about the nature of the danger. A park ranger surprised us by telling of two people killed beyond that point only a few months earlier. It was a simple matter, actually. They ignored the sign and went around the barricade. They stepped on a loose slide and were carried over the edge to death.

One of the children blurted something like, "Couldn't you do anything about it?"

The ranger could have, with justification, replied something like this: "Well, I suppose we could just keep everyone out of the park and not let them get anywhere near the mountain. Nobody would get killed here, but nobody would enjoy the mountain, either. If we let people in, they obey the rules and take our warnings. If they don't, there's nothing more we can do but pick up their bodies.

"When they deliberately ignored our warning, and when they decided to go beyond the barrier, there were just no safety devices left to save them. The sign warned them, and the barrier got them to pause. That's about all it could do, and that's all it was ever meant to do."

Christ's sacrifice is meant to give to spiritually dead people spiritual life, which is eternal. It does. The presence of Christ and the work of the Holy Spirit in our lives are meant to give us a continual experience with salvation. Having come to life in Christ and having become fully knowledgeable in the truth, if we should also deliberately persist in sinning and if there is no more sacrifice available for that sinning, what then? "Only a fearful expectation of judgment and of a raging fire that will consume the enemies of God" (v. 27).

When no sacrifice is available for this sinning, this sinning is not forgiven and we cannot experience the healing that would come from forgiveness. We cannot, and will not, escape the consequences of that sinning.

That is a frightful expectation of judgment. That judgment burns like a fire and consumes all it burns. Sin is found to be sin. Unrepented sin is found unrepented and unforgivable. There is, then, no salvation from the consequences of those sins. The consequence is suffered.

Any exceptions? Any mitigation of the sentence? Unthinkable. Consider the past. The Law of Moses was good, but it was nothing in comparison with the new covenant in God's Son. Yet, under the Law, all it took to condemn a violator was "the testimony of two or three witnesses" (v. 28). Such "dies without mercy."

"How much worse punishment do you think will be deserved by the man who . . ." violates the new covenant?

The writer asked, "How much more severely do you think a man deserves to be punished who has trampled the Son of God underfoot, who has treated as an unholy thing the blood of the covenant that sanctified him, and who has insulted the Spirit of grace?" (v. 29). The acts themselves are witnesses to the sins: (1) spurning the Son of God; (2) profaning the blood of the covenant; and (3) outraging the Spirit of grace. Note the similarity to the previous warning, to those who are "crucifying the Son of God all over again and subjecting him to public disgrace" (6:6).

This cannot and will not be tolerated, because of the very nature of spiritual reality. There is no God if such things can be successfully done to what we had thought of as God. The Creator, who made all things good and in order, will one day complete his creation by returning the good and reordering things.

And this is what the author meant in quoting the Law of Moses, "Vengeance is mine, I will repay" (Deut. 32), and also, "The Lord will judge his people."

Do not read human emotion into "vengeance" and "repay." God had to use man's language in talking to man, even about his own actions. These are equivalent and not exact terms. God's action is both morally better and the consequences worse than man's. Having quoted the Old Testament doctrine, the writer added this insightful observation: "It is a dreadful thing to fall into the hands of the living God" (v. 31).

For years I thought this said, "the angry God." I suspect now, that I was thinking more of that famous sermon of Jonathan Edwards, "Sinners in the Hands of an Angry God." I had learned that there are certain people you just don't get angry at you because they have the power to finish you off.

This makes it worse: God isn't angry.

We can speak of God as being "angry" of course, but that is a manner of speaking, using man's language for God's action. And there are times when God acts in a mode that can only be identified as "anger." But this is worse: God is living. Anger can cool off. We can remove the cause of anger. We can escape anger. But God always lives. Nothing will ever change that. We can never escape the consequences from the living God.

When we are spiritually alive and living our salvation, the living God keeps our salvation active and we keep living salvation and keep being saved.

When we persist in deliberate sinning, the living God deals with that sinning. A fearful thing!

STEPPING OUT Hebrews 10:32-39

We will not walk away, then, but we will draw near. Drawing near to God in worship and fellowship enables us to step out in action and work.

Confidence comes from spiritual victories. Let's persist in those victories. As we do, we work our faith. In working our faith, we take possession of our souls. That's stepping out in spiritual experience, drawing near to God so we can go on in life.

The writer reminded the Hebrews of their early, positive experiences. "Remember those earlier days" (10:32).

Those were "the good ol' days," some might have responded. That is a curious expression, because "the good ol' days" weren't usually really good. Rather, if there be any truth to it at all, there was something good within those days. Not the time, but the experience is the point.

I could refer to the 1930s as the good ol' days. The Great Depression, yes, but more significant, it was the years of my happy childhood in a loving family.

I was born the year following the collapse of the stock market and grew up in the depression. But I never knew it. I sustained grief and strife, I suppose, but I experienced giving and love. To learn of the economic conditions of the 30s, I had to study historical records. What I remember are the social and spiritual conditions of our family. They weren't so much the good ol' days, then, but the good ol' folks.

That's what, spiritually, the writer wanted his readers to

keep in mind, his word meaning literally "to remember again." That they had forgotten in practice those days was much of the problem. The challenge was to recall them, dig them up from the archives and set them up as working documents.

So it isn't the days or the things of the days we need to keep in mind, but the experiences. Sadly, some Christians remember only superficial wrappings of those days of spiritual victories when they need to recall the substance.

This, I suspect, is at the root of much resistance to change and insistence on the way we have always done it. While I was speaking at a Bible conference near Seattle, I heard the director criticize a college music group for its modern music. The good ol' hymns of the faith are what he demanded.

When he stated the list of songs he approved, I recognized that none were hymns and none were old. They were gospel songs and date no earlier than his own youth.

I don't gainsay for a moment what those songs mean to him. But he had forgotten that those songs were modern music in the days he learned them. This man was really asking the kids to have his experience and, by so doing, was in danger of denying them their own. Tragically, for some older Christians those gospel songs are all that remains of their spiritual experience. Singing them is more a memorial than a renewal.

It would be a helpful device to sing again those songs. But we need to recall the tears with which we first sang them, the struggles endured and the victories won.

The conditions threatened, but the victory was great.

The writer of Hebrews reminded his readers of those earlier days when they "stood [their] ground in a great contest in the face of suffering. Sometimes [they] were publicly exposed to insult and persecution; at other times [they] stood side by side with those who were so treated" (10:32, 33).

He reminded them not of a simple hard time. It was a fierce contest to see who would win. Not some rough moments; they experienced the deepest agony, but they came through it. They were not bystanders, but participants. The literal language suggests that they were put on public display and made a spectacle before the crowds.

Rather than disassociating themselves from their brothers who had become political prisoners, they exercised compassion on them. When their property was confiscated, it became a joyful event.

The writer didn't call on them to abdicate earthly possessions as of no value. He affirmed their value as gifts from the Creator, but asserted that there is greater value still.

One of the characteristics of the Epistle to the Hebrews is its honest celebration of the goodness of God's creations on earth. Another is its accurate revelation of the better things beyond this imperfect earth. It's a good life, but it is growing into one greater still. The writer urged them, "So do not throw away your confidence; it will be richly rewarded" (v. 35).

Confidence, again, means "with-faith." Recent generations have sought to instill fear, caution, and humility (even humiliation). The contemporary generation claims boldness, abandon, and arrogance. Neither understands confidence. Confidence means you know what to do and how to do it; you know what you're doing and why you're doing it. It means you know where you're going, and you'll know when you get there. It means you know what you're after, and you'll know when you get it.

Confidence is the opposite of arrogance. Arrogance precedes a fall; confidence prevents falling.

Accept confidence as God's gift. Then use it productively. Recalling spiritual victories of the past builds confidence, the writer stressed. Confidence, he assured us, has a great reward.

The writer's word is formed from one root meaning "hire" and another meaning "pay." Fiscal experts refer to things like this as "return on investment."

For the Christian believer, confidence is doing the will of God and receiving what is promised. For this, the writer said we "need to persevere" (v. 36).

Our need to persist is not, he said, vague. We need not fear the Coming One who will not tarry, described by Habakkuk (2:3, 4). Because: "the righteous will live by his faith."

The one who is made righteous by God is made to live from within the resources of his faith. If we who have been so made righteous should shrink back, "my soul has no pleasure in him."

While the prophet warns, the author remains confident: "But we are not of those who shrink back and are destroyed, but of those who have faith and keep their souls" (Heb. 10:39, RSV).

Maturing believers who actively practice their faith draw near rather than shrinking back. They do not walk away, they step out.

To walk away, to shrink back, is to choose destruction. The language does not present destruction as what the shrinker happens to be left with. The act of shrinking is followed separately by a second action of being destroyed. To shrink, at least here, implies the decision to withdraw or pull back from.

The boxer who pulls his punches is the one most likely to be knocked out. He who keeps his hands and arms over his face in protection will be most surely knocked out. To pull back from the opponent is to back into defeat.

When faced with moral danger, we must face the danger spiritually. It is the safest as well as the only effective thing to do. We must make decisions and choices. There is no avoiding them.

The writer assured his readers that those of faith "keep their souls" or do so "to the saving of their souls." Rather than using the possessive "have faith," he spoke of those who were "of faith." The successful believer spends his faith and so gains his soul.

Rather than betraying a salvation-by-works misconception, the writer rightly conceived of a working salvation. Salvation not only rescues the soul from sin, but delivers it to righteousness.

Today we speak of "having a grip on things," or "having things under control." Paul spoke of *obtaining* salvation (1 Thess. 5:9, RSV) and the glory of the Lord (2 Thess. 2:14, RSV), the same word used in Hebrews.

He was speaking of healthy souls, believers who have grown strong, not fat. What we have learned about bodily health and physical fitness provides an analogy for spiritual experience. The body mass we need is muscle tissue, not fat cells. In a less knowledgeable age they assumed fatness to be healthy. We know better now.

Yet, we seem to accept it more in physiology than in spiritual thought. The Church of our age and society is critically infected with an existential disease of epidemic proportions. We suffer from spiritual malnutrition complicated by religious obesity. The more we hunger for spiritual nourishment, the more we gorge ourselves on religious junk food. We grow heavy, not healthy—fat, not strong.

For many years I refused to look into those three-sided mirrors in clothing stores. Not only did I fill all sides, there was no escaping the reflection since it came at me from all sides. The clerks, politically, referred to "the mature gentleman," "a full body," "the substantial look." The terms didn't change the fact. I wasn't strong. I wasn't healthy. I was fat—and ashamed. And I was heading for an early death.

I chose to lose weight, and divested myself of seventy pounds.

Now, I not only have a smaller diet but a better diet. It is funny now. No one would believe the foods I had been eating and didn't even like. I now taste food. I now enjoy food. Before, I enjoyed eating.

Let each of us stand in front of the biblical mirror with the Holy Spirit's commentary. Look at the soul. Don't be impressed by bulk. Be suspicious of it. Poke it. Pinch it. Is it flabby or hard? Does it lift up or only fill out?

What about all this we carry around? How much of it is religious pretense and how much spiritual reality? Religion is what you do when you are not spiritual.

Review the calendar for the last month. How much time is marked out for church, religion, and things of that nature? How much of it was only occupied by religious activity? And how much was used for spiritual experience?

Four Sunday morning and four Sunday evening services. How much of that was worship, how much growth? How have you changed, and what have you produced?

Are we stepping out confidently and receiving the reward of God's will and what he promised? Are we living actively by faith and taking full possession of our souls?

I shall recall those early victories and regain my confidence.

SIX

BUILD UP, LEST YOU FALL APART
HEBREWS 12:12-17

On a hot, humid day in late August, the high school team plods down the street. They hardly act like a team now, but they were members of last year's team and now are prospective members of this year's.

The coach calls it jogging, conditioning, runs. Wearing themselves out before they have played the first game, doing something now they will never do then.

The coach put it to them the first day of football camp:

> You guys think you're tough just because you're big. Heavy isn't the same thing as strong. Sure, you can push your way through the ninth grade boys in the hall. But when you get out there on that field, you're going to line up against real men—at least as big and heavy as you. You've got to build yourselves up now so you don't fall apart when we need you. You've got to be in top shape or you'll never last. You have to prepare for the worst when things are the best. When the games start, we'll give all our attention to the winning. The time will come to put out. Now's the time to build up.

"Build up, lest you fall apart." With warnings and exhortations not unlike those of a coach, the writer of Hebrews has been challenging us to the active practice of our spiritual faith.

Having expressed four of the exhortations and all five warnings, he climaxed the appeal with the final exhortation. He purposed so strongly and reasoned so skillfully that it created a specific effect.

The warnings are unforgettably implied in the language of the fifth exhortation: "Build up, lest you fall apart." Just as top physical condition is created by physical conditioning, we can expect top spiritual condition to result from spiritual conditioning.

If we do not condition ourselves spiritually, the pressures of this world will cause us to fall apart. If we are not in top spiritual condition then the greatest pressure, when applied, will crush us.

No Christian believer can anticipate how great will be the pressure he will encounter in the future. All we can do is prepare for the worst. We are then prepared for everything.

No experienced football player can know how much running another mile in training will help him the last game of the coming season. There is no way he can anticipate the need or measure the exercise's value, but no building up is ever wasted.

The athlete has done one hundred push-ups. Should he do another ten? Not "should," but "can" is the question. If he can, he should.

The next day he may be able to do 110 because the day before he really tried. In trying, he built up his muscles so that the next time he accomplishes it.

Athletes wear themselves out in training so they never wear down in performance. As the coach said, "Now's the time to build up. The time will come to put out. When it does, we want to be sure we haven't given out."

The writer of Hebrews challenged the believers to active faith. Faith is not a possession. It is an activity, an experience. Ultimately, our spiritual maturity depends upon the work of the Holy Spirit, whose work becomes effective as we take action. For success to come, the condition for success must exist. The condition comes from conditioning. The conditioning is accomplished by the one who will experience the condition and accomplish the success.

New birth into eternal life is a gift of God. The living of eternal life is the experience of the born-again.

All God told Adam and Eve about dominating the world and

being fruitful is centrally true of our spiritual welfare. God created the world; and there is no more creation of that kind. But God's principal creation lives to be creative with the creation from which God now rests. It is up to us because the Creator left it to us.

When the Redeemer recreated us, it was to build up the life he gave. To build ourselves up is to affirm God's gift by using it. To leave this also to God is to neglect the gift. It is impossible to escape the consequences of such neglect.

For the last exhortation, the writer encouraged rebuilding spiritual strength (v. 12), moving by straight steps (v. 13), and the two-dimensional responsibility of pressing on in our relationships and overseeing the spiritual health of others (vv. 14-17).

We are to build up to top spiritual condition by conditioning ourselves spiritually. Otherwise, the pressures of this world will cause us to fall apart.

REBUILDING SPIRITUAL STRENGTH *Hebrews 12:12*

This epistle has already said a lot about maturing, growing, and strengthening. These objectives must themselves produce results still more far-reaching. They describe changes in the readers who are so equipped to reach others and change them. Strength in the reader, yes. But that strength—strengthening—enables service or ministry.

With this section, the writer began his exhortations to the readers to become effective leaders of fellow believers, since we minister to others best by building ourselves up into strong and able ministers.

Exercise yourself, and take care of yourself. Use your strength to obtain the full grace of God, he said as the last formal exhortation: "Therefore, strengthen your feeble arms and weak knees. Make level paths for your feet" (vv. 12, 13).

Using the figures of the human body, the writer drew the analogy between physical fitness and strong spiritual condition. Although the ability he valued also related to manual labor, he seemed to have more immediately in mind the figure of an athlete. One can envision the runner with his full body committed to the task.

Instructions are issued for hands, knees, and feet, all crucial to effective running. If the writer had known something about the cardiovascular system, the Spirit could have put into his mind also the importance of top condition for the heart and lungs. It doesn't take much imagination to extend the biblical figure to these.

Arms, legs, and feet must be in top physical condition for the body to function effectively. Far from enjoying top spiritual condition, the readers had sustained deterioration from the health of early growth.

The standard method of strengthening muscles is to exercise them. This means, first, using the muscles in the way they must be used to perform an act for which they are not yet ready, by way of preparation. The other sense is actually doing these acts as a regular activity, and regularly succeeding through performance.

Yet, preparation and performance are not totally distinct. We cannot prepare without actual performance, and each actual performance is preparation for greater performance.

A runner exercises his or her running muscles before the run, but then exercises the muscles in order to run. A physician practices medical arts as a medical student and intern. Then a state issues a license to practice medicine. The practice and exercise of preparation and performance are not entirely distinct but are decidedly related.

Can we practice ministry? Can we exercise spiritually? Yes. But preparation for performance is normal and essential, not merely usual and important.

Football teams prepare for scheduled games by scrimmages. Marathoners run at least fifty miles a week for at least two months before each event, with a twenty-mile run weekly, to approach the 26.2 miles of the actual event. No combat invasion is launched without its having been dry-run until the maneuver can be done in the soldiers' sleep. Ten hour practice days are not unusual for serious musicians.

I fail to see it an unspiritual thing to practice spiritual acts. Thinking through a public prayer so it can be understood by the congregation that will hear it is not what causes insincerity. Dry-running a witness opportunity isn't fakery. I don't feel dishonest when I make myself act friendly toward a hostile stranger—especially when friendship results.

The Book of Psalms displays the reasonableness and effectiveness of priming the spiritual pump with religious water until the Living Water flows. I repeat the psalmists' prayers until the Spirit gives me my own. I may say a prayer until I can pray. Preparation for physical performance is very often entirely mental. We need encouragement.

It seems the writer understood his readers needed emotional encouragement about as much as anything: "Lift those drooping hands. Lock your knees into place. Put those feet one in front of another."

Encouragement comes by at least three routes. We can *receive* encouragement through such exhortations as we read in this epistle or such as kind brothers and sisters speak to us. But don't count on it. Others have their problems, too, and it's sometimes at the same time as we are having ours.

Second, we can *take* encouragement. That is to say, our brothers and sisters don't need to verbalize encouragement. We can see in their lives the good things we need and, then, choose to take encouragement upon seeing them. I wonder if this kind isn't really the better source. It allows our friends to concentrate their attention upon others who need it more, and it allows us to be responsible about our own lives.

Third, we can *give* encouragement. When we are depressed and no one seems concerned enough to encourage us, we can encourage ourselves. We can choose to be encouraged. We can go out and find someone we think needs the same encouragement we do. Having done so, we can say to ourselves, "Did you hear what you just said? Now, do it for yourself."

Still other times some assigned task is such that no preparation was possible. We feel encouraged enough anyway, but it seems unreasonable to expect success. Another way to express such feelings is as "faith in God" or "the gift of confidence."

I often find another biblical term to be more appropriate: obedience. Often I have longed for a more profound faith when the immediate need was simple obedience.

We must not thoughtlessly and needlessly ask God, "Give me strength!" We should develop the strength, or ask God to help us use well the strength we have already developed for the task at hand.

It may seem arrogant to say, "God, I have the strength; guide me as I use it." It's also outrageous to say, "God, I don't have the strength because I didn't develop it when you told me to—so just give it to me, anyway."

At other times, God confronts us with tasks for which we have no previous strength or skill and for which there is no source other than the performance of the task itself. Then, we should perform. God will give the strength and skill. This gift, however, need not be expected as a divine intervention since it is more likely to be a natural provision.

The example most meaningful to me is the matter of teaching. I had to learn about teaching in order to begin teaching. When I began to teach, I really learned about teaching as well as what I was teaching. Having been a teacher for some time, I began to forget some things and to recognize others I hadn't learned about. I became a student again and, as a result, was further prepared to teach.

A student stops learning if he doesn't start teaching what he has learned. A teacher stops teaching if she doesn't start learning more about what she has been teaching. They are forever student teachers and teaching students.

For this reason, I strongly encourage churches to require this interaction for both students and teachers. Every Christian who has learned anything at all about the Bible and Christian life can—and should—teach someone, something, sometime about what he has learned. If he can't, he hasn't learned. If he has learned and doesn't, he'll forget.

Every teacher should pursue a planned program of learning, perhaps a once-a-month weeknight teacher training class for Sunday school teachers. At least as important are sabbaticals from regular teaching to become a Sunday school student once again for a while. If he isn't willing to do that, he hasn't been teaching. If he has been teaching and doesn't, he won't really teach much longer.

Strengthening, in spiritual reality, results from a balanced relationship between preparation and performance.

MOVING BY STRAIGHT STEPS Hebrews 12:13

"Make straight tracks for your feet" literally expresses the exhortation.

In life, as in running, one does not normally choose his own surface. He negotiates whatever surface he encounters. He must do it with a skill in which runners are trained. Even when a running track has been constructed, the runner must put his feet down efficiently and effectively.

Not only a vivid illustration from modern running, the writer's language shows this sense. The word "paths" does not indicate a constructed roadway or previously worn-smooth surface, but the tracks created by putting one's foot onto the surface of the course one takes.

Moreover, "straight" or "level" describes right order or proper condition rather than a geometric figure such as a straight line. So, again, arms and legs are to be strengthened.

Running efficiently is more complex than impact on such external things as the surface. Also at stake is the effect upon the runner, such internal factors as preserving strength and avoiding injury.

Motion and strain that do not produce movement cause premature and unnecessary fatigue. The spiritual performer, like the runner, is prepared to accept being used up when he has accomplished something worthwhile. But neither wants to be worn out by unproductive motion. In that case, everything is given out and nothing is gained.

Inefficient motor coordination in running compounds itself so that it eventually degenerates further into ineffectiveness, so severe that we can run no longer because we have actually injured ourselves. How an athlete runs and how a child of God acts determines how they build themselves up. This, in turn, decides whether the one wins and the other succeeds.

The writer, in using these analogies, wasn't referring to our chancing upon easy convenient happenstances. Distances aren't run that way, nor is life so lived. Not where the Christian runs, but how he runs wherever it is he is given to run determines success.

Spirituality is essentially an attitude. However much the physical world may be used and appreciated, our activity is essentially a matter of the spirit. With our individual spirits in fellowship with the Holy Spirit, we begin with the motives and goals of the spirit. We proceed as a spirit, using spiritual guidelines and standards. We conclude with the spirit's benefit above all, having accomplished spiritual things in a spiritual manner for spiritual purposes.

Take such a physical activity as eating. What can be more

physical than that? Surely, this is one activity a Christian is allowed to perform without worrying about being spiritual.

Not so. The animals eat quite well without doing it spiritually. But we are persons, not animals. We are spirits, even though clothed in bodies. Humans ought to—Christians can and must—feed their bodies material food in a spiritual manner for the sake of the spirit.

Whether one eats to live or lives to eat is the difference in attitudes. Bodies can be nourished and strengthened to be more efficient vehicles of the spirit. Tasting with sensuous pleasure the fruit of God's good earth can allow us to rejoice at his provision and celebrate the bounty of his creation.

I am not suggesting that Christian families serve only "evangelically kosher food," or confine dinner conversation to quoting Scripture with a family Bible for a centerpiece. That's religion; we're talking about spirituality. Spirituality is not pseudo piety.

And where have we heard that all sex is dirty and that for Christians, who are safely married, it is just something to tolerate? To take seriously some preachers, and parents who parrot them, one has the picture of God being a lecherous old man suspiciously spying on young people lest two of them have fun he can't. After marriage, it is different. God and the angels look the other way when the bedroom door is closed.

Finding it impossible, or at least frustrating, to be total abstainers from sexual activity and certainly lacking any doctrine of sexuality, sex seems to be the moral Achilles' heel of otherwise religiously perfect church members. For many nice church boys, anything goes so long as you don't go all the way with a good Christian girl. Not a few Christian husbands exploit their wives for self-gratification and treat them as legal and cheap "kept" women rather than the beloved they seek to please.

There is such a thing, I am convinced, as a Christian husband and wife engaging in sex in a way that isn't a spiritual experience. It seems to me that mutual fulfillment, not self-gratification, would be that. I don't suggest that marital sex be in a candlelit room in front of a picture of Jesus with gospel records playing softly in the background. Expressions of love that thrill the spirit must also bring ecstatic pleasure to their bodies. The neurological release for the body in physical acts creates a refreshing of spirits for the Spirit-led lovers.

And God, who does look on, smiles at the two he made to become one, acting out their oneness. Because he smiles, the angels sing. God, who is Spirit, is satisfied with his creation when bodies he created live as spirits.

In ways such as these, the Christian, actively practicing his faith, lives spiritually in a body on the earth. He refuses to view anything as secular, but transforms everything into the sacred. He finds things considered secular, with no reference to God and his purpose for them, and redeems them for God's glory.

The active Christian is careful how he puts his feet down in the race. For example, she is a high school English teacher, and he is an elementary school teacher. Both live vibrant spiritual lives so that their students see, though they might not yet understand, Christ in them.

And they teach as Christian teachers, whether in public or Christian schools. They act professionally in a spiritual manner.

She values the Bible as fine literature as well as divine Scripture. She is effective in teaching methods and treats all students fairly and honestly.

He shows spiritual dimensions in all the class studies and is concerned with the students' learning and is kind and gentle in his treatment.

If it seems an accomplishment to do secular work in a spiritual manner, it is especially so when a person succeeds in doing religious work in a spiritual way.

God expects the man employed as a salesman all week to serve him throughout the week as well as on weekends. We need to hear more about the professional Christian worker serving the Lord full-time. It isn't the amount of time spent on the job, but the job being dedicated to serving the Lord. We need to be sure the work accomplishes ministry goals rather than merely playing a professional role.

Fit and strong arms, legs, and feet are together essential for successful running. Some joggers seem to think it is enough to develop only good leg muscles, and then wonder why they move so inefficiently and why they tire so quickly. The body is a marvelous system in which one part supports the others. If unusual demands are made on the legs, proportionate strain will be sustained in the upper body. Push-ups and sit-ups are also part of running.

Balance and proportion are very important in the spiritual life, also. We must insist upon this for ourselves to overcome the influence of single-issue politics, special interest organizations, professional specialization, and denominational exclusiveness.

How can I pray meaningfully without feeling a need to return to the Scriptures for richer material and deeper understanding? And how can I study Scripture productively without sensing a need to pray about what I have learned and to pray in the spirit of the biblical prayers? I suspect if I have not balanced prayer and Bible reading in my private life, neither becomes a part of my experience and both are mere exercises.

If God has given unusual skill in personal evangelism to someone, it seems reasonable for him to expect to spend unusual time in winning souls and to receive unusual results. But I counsel such a person to take a close look at his fellowship with brothers and sisters and measure both his investment in it and growth because of it. If he doesn't experience refreshing personal growth from his fellowship, he is unlikely to remain successful as a soul-winner.

And concerning world missions, are souls of varying values, depending upon their geographical proximity to the witness? Or, does charity begin overseas?

So, too, the Barnabas-type believer, who is especially used by the Spirit to encourage his brothers and sisters, shouldn't spend all his time with them. Perhaps he should go along with the evangelist and help bring strangers into the family he nurtures so well.

Is a person so preoccupied with the local church that he never lifts his eyes to the universal Church? Or is the Church as an ideal what spoils his patience with the churches?

I worry about a politician who puts all his energy into such a needed thing as finding and exposing communists in American government. He soon, like any other totalitarian, finds "communists" who aren't even there. I worry also about a psychiatric professional who works overtime in the mental hospital, lives on the grounds, and uses other staff members as his total social outlet. How can such a person ever recognize a normal person?

And I worry about the Christian who locks himself into one, highly specific spiritual enterprise. Perhaps one can't get too much of a good thing, but one can get so much of one good thing that he doesn't get enough of other good things. When that happens, the good thing we had loses its connection with the system of spiritual reality, and we lose what we thought we had.

When God assigns a specialized ministry, we should concentrate on it and not abandon all others. More than a few itinerant evangelists have done great harm to local congregations by their insensitivity. Some foreign missionaries, by furlough time, have forgotten how to communicate in the home culture.

If there be any ministry that is, by definition, one of balance and comprehensiveness, it is the office of pastor. A shepherd feeds and leads his sheep, ministering to individuals in family and community. The pastor is a father among fathers in a family of families.

Lest they be known as "only a pastor," many seek some singular distinction, which destroys their authenticity and leaves them something less than a pastor. Balance. That's the word. And if your pastor is an adequate pastor, that's quite enough. Don't expect him to be an outstanding something else.

How, then, do we strengthen again spiritual arms, legs, and feet? How do we proportion spiritual strength?

Identify all the components of Christian experience, all parts of our soul. Start with the Bible, and validate it by the experience of more mature believers. Measure the dimensions in terms of height, depth, breadth, and length. Check proportions relative to each. Test their balance. Inspect the relationships.

Then stand back and view the totality. Ask, "What is the quantity and quality of my spiritual experience? How does it balance?"

Although the formal warnings have been laid down, even the final exhortation comes with its implied warnings: "Make level paths for your feet, so that the lame may not be disabled, but rather healed" (v. 13).

Bad enough that one is injured by falling behind in his growth. If he doesn't bring about healing by building himself up, those arms, legs, and feet will become completely disjointed.

Although the word is often used also for other kinds of turning aside, this medical sense accords with the body metaphor. Failure to take care of oneself, we have already observed, is an invitation to permanent and irreversible injury—disablement.

The sense continues the writer's theme. As long as it is called today, we can build up; tomorrow is falling apart.

PRESSING ON AND OVERSEEING Hebrews 12:14-17

A weight lifting champion who wouldn't trouble himself to lift a helpless child from danger would show how worthless his skills, which otherwise would have been applauded, really are. A body is built up not to be admired but to be used.

Spiritual strength and the skill to use it, in themselves, imply a mandate to use them productively. If implications had been enough, the Hebrews would not have been falling apart and needing to be rebuilt. Strength they had developed at the outset had since atrophied from inactivity.

The Hebrews needed further exhortations, so the writer extended the fifth to this purpose. Rebuilding spiritual strength and moving by straight steps enable the maturing believer to press on in spiritual experience and to take leadership.

"Strengthen your weak arms and legs. Put your feet down right. Now, press on to peace with men and holiness before God, and watch over the health of others." These two goals confront the growing believer. In the writer's words: "Make every effort to live in peace with all men and to be holy; without holiness no one will see the Lord" (v. 14).

That we should desire peace with men and holiness before the Lord we can grasp without difficulty.

The words "make every effort" sound strong until we recall the meanings of peace and holiness. Then it not only makes sense, but it works. Peace identifies the positive state of good relationships, which must be constructed, not just the absence of strife, peace describes relationships working productively. Holiness identifies separation from sin and evil, and being like God. It, too, is something we work at to attain. The saved person becoming holy actively achieves holiness by the grace of God rather than passively receiving it by some indulgence of God.

Peace and holiness are not pictured as quantities we create directly. We allow, foster, and even create the conditions from

which these result as qualities of relationships we build. We
create the conditions under which peace is constructed. We re-
pudiate sin, of which we must be rid, so the Spirit can sanctify
the life actively yielded to his control.

Being familiar with the Hebrew Scriptures, the readers
would respond to this mention of peace within the framework
of the ancient concept. *Shalom* was a word so basic to Hebrew
thought-form that no translation can be adequate. Complete
welfare and perfect health are among the closer English approaches to the depth of its meaning.

A Hebrew, pronouncing *shalom* upon one he met, committed
himself to the creation and sustenance of what he said. He
promised—something more than a wish. When the person
greeted responded in kind, the two had, by doing so, made a
binding covenant which worked both as an obligation and a
responsibility.

The one felt responsible for the other. He felt obliged to himself because he had committed himself to peace. Unfaithfulness
would risk not only social relations but personal integrity.

Peace with men and holiness before the Lord beckon from
the horizon as goals toward which we are always pressing. This
verb, "follow after," or sometimes translated "make every effort" which jars the naive, is most often used in a negative sense
in the Bible. When people of the world "followed after" Christians to persecute them, they were serious and meant business.
Equally serious, and as much a matter of business, is the Christian's task to "follow after" such qualities as love, goodness,
righteousness, godliness, and faith. Whether used in a negative
or positive sense, good or bad, these were crucial goals to be
reached at all costs.

The basic meaning of the word is "hasten, run, and press on."
Its application is "pursue, strive for, seek after, or aspire to."

The Apostle Paul used this strong word well in Philippians:
"I *press on* to take hold of that for which Christ Jesus took told
of me. I *press on* toward the goal to win the prize for which God
has called me heavenward in Christ Jesus" (Phil. 3:12, 14).

The writer of Hebrews exhorted his readers to press on to
peace with men and holiness before God. He wanted them to
do everything within their power to create these wholesome
relationships.

Holiness, again, is spiritual experience rather than religious conformity. So, too, peace is personal experience rather than social conformity. Some so-called "peacemakers" often manipulate people into a negotiated cessation of hostilities. Then they label it peace. Individuals remain fierce enemies, and hostilities erupt the moment one thinks he can defeat the other without undue harm to himself.

That's not peace. Yet it is what we often settle for. This is not only dishonest, but worthless. In many cases, it would be better to have it out and get it over with so we can get on to other things. That pseudo-peace deepens pain and prolongs agony.

Faithful Christians accomplish peace far more often and far better than unbelievers, to be sure. We have, indeed, the only real peace. Still, I believe many ungodly, secular people do better at fostering peace than some religious people—even Christians, if overly religious.

Reflect on the euphemisms used for this artificial nonsense. Smoothing things over—steadying the boat—stilling the waves—making peace—pouring oil on troubled waters—doing something to make everyone happy.

Smoothing a cosmetic over diseased skin may escape social embarrassment, but it makes the disease tolerable. A steadied boat can sink as quickly. Stilled waves can't wash the beach. Making peace is like making love—neither is what it pretends. Enough oil could calm the lake, but who wants to swim in oil? We don't need artificial things to make people happy, but reality to create joy.

I know peacemakers who are quite skilled at these things, but they take off before fighting breaks out again so they can kid themselves they had accomplished something.

Building peace bogs down when we deny we have differences or problems. We must courageously seek out differences and identify them honestly. We must invite the differing party to explain and support his perspective, and listen receptively. We must ask for permission to present our perspective. We must refuse to regard differences of expression as differences of substance.

Not infrequently, differences have either disappeared by this step or they are recognized as being of no significance. When the two parties agree on this, we can expect that some other problems between them will be settled also.

On the other hand, understanding the differences could unearth problems that would never have surfaced if no one had known or cared. Yet, it will be just that much easier to resolve them.

Some differences will never be reconciled, and some problems will never be solved.But we must learn to live with differences and different people, to live with problems and problem people.

There's an indescribable thrill that comes from learning to live and work with people with whom we have serious differences. Even the lost might find their way together if they never differ.

A genius of the Christian experience is to thrive by the rigors of such living. It toughens and enriches.

Leadership responsibility for his readers becomes intense as the writer of Hebrews encouraged his readers to avoid these dangers within the Body of Christ:

> See to it that no one misses the grace of God and that no biter root grows up to cause trouble and defile many. See that no one is sexually immoral, or is godless like Esau, who for a single meal sold his inheritance rights as the oldest son (vv. 16, 17).

From the imperative, "See to it," I picture the Christian leader with a good set of eyes kept open. He was not to let those for whom he cared out of his sight. Other writers used the word in contexts of "take heed," "mark," "look on," and "consider."

The Apostle Peter instructed leaders: "Be shepherds of God's flock that is under your care, *serving as overseers*" (1 Peter 5:2). There it is "exercise the responsibility of oversight."

This exhortation stands defiantly against today's popular advice: "Don't get involved," "Don't interfere," "Mind your own business," "Stay out of other people's affairs." These remarks pretend to be assertions of others' freedom, but they are betrayals of their own irresponsibility and indifference.

We desire freedom for every person, and it is precisely because we are our brothers' keepers that we want to see them free from sin so they can be all that God made them to be. When we pull a drowning child from the water, we give him the freedom to live. Enslavement under sin is certainly not freedom.

My first visit to see a halfway house for drug addicts was to a place on Chicago's southside. A fourteen-year-old girl told the group she was going to leave and became frustrated by their disagreement and criticism. "It's my life! Why are you so mad?"

A group member replied calmly but intensely, "Because, you silly thing, we care more about you than you do!"

One trait of a maturing, active Christian is that he actually cares more about his immature, inactive brothers than they care about themselves. He never takes his eyes off them. He insures that none straggle behind the grace of God.

I caution against jumping to conclusions about the meaning of this passage. The writer said nothing here about "falling from grace" in the sense of departing entirely from the sphere in which God's grace operates. Part of the problem in our understanding it is our having confined the concept of grace to redemptive grace and not going on to think of preserving grace and then to growing grace. The convenient definition of "unmerited favor" is too restricted.

God's grace is God's care for his children. Our Lord's gracious care is what only God can do. It is God's provision for normal spiritual living.

The verb "misses" is sometimes translated something like "fail to obtain," with the sense of failing to keep up with the grace of God. Paul described the results of sin as to *"fall short* of the glory of God" (Romans 3:23), and wanted the Corinthians to *"come behind* in no gift" (1 Corinthians 1:7). The writer of Hebrews warned about those who "should seem *to come short* of" God's rest (4:1, KJV) and spoke of the faithful who were plundered of material things and left "destitute" (11:37) of what was rightfully theirs.

A Hebrew word of the same sense is used by the prophet Micah in his promise that God "will assemble the *lame*" (Micah 4:6). Moffatt puts it, "I will collect the *stragglers.*" Those of Israel became lame by straggling behind the covenant promises.

The safest place to be in combat is on the front line directly facing the enemy. The most dangerous place is straggling behind the advancing forces where one can't see the enemy.

For this reason, a serious part of my training as a military police officer was the course entitled "Straggler Collection." We were instructed to keep our men constantly on patrol just behind the FEBA (forward edge of the battle area) to keep an eye out for troops who had fallen behind the advancing lines. Whether consciously deserting, confused by fear, or helplessly wounded, they were equally in fatal danger. The enemy leaves snipers, hiding quietly in place, when he retreats. Others infiltrate our lines. With the firepower moved forward and stragglers unalert, the snipers pick them off, one by one. How frightening to learn the enemy regards them as targets of opportunity.

MPs return stragglers to their units, and the commanders put them on the line where it is safest. The soldier on the line has skilled leadership, competent support, excellent resources, and adequate reenforcement. He knows where the enemy is and who is his commander. He knows, too, where he stands and where he is going.

The safest and the most successful Christian is he who is directly facing the enemy, in fellowship with alert, active brothers, constantly calling upon God for grace to do what he cannot do in himself.

The victorious Christian soldier tolerates no illusions about moral defensiveness. He values defense on every side against the influence of evil.

A Christian doesn't wait for the enemy to attack. He takes the initiative and goes on to the offensive.

The battle is often closer to home than a battlefield scene might depict it. An acquaintance ridicules an absent third person, a fellow Christian, for her moral and religious values and standards. What are we to do?

We can remain silent and pray. That's always nice. We might work the conversation around to a safer subject. Perhaps if we feel special responsibility, we can later inform the third person and leave it to her.

If the conversation should come to be directed toward you, there is always the possibility of disavowing any identification or implication. You can claim that the absent sister probably takes things a little far and might be something of a fanatic. But not you, of course. You take your religion seriously, but you also know when to leave it out of things.

Such defensive tactics have the value of being well rehearsed and fully supported by precedent. But how would we take the offense in such a situation? What if we were to say: "I know that person. She's my sister in Christ. I think I can explain what she is trying to tell and show you. I share her values and standards, whatever differences we might have about them." I can predict what would happen. I've seen it happen a number of times. For some, the response would be a willingness to learn. It would change the initial assault into a strange invitation for explanation. It might be unreasonable to expect open repentance of the attacker then and there. But, surely, it moves in that direction.

Sometimes the attacker withdraws, which is often an admission that the complaint was not all that serious. What a shame if we should take such people seriously and become defensive against aimless wind that wasn't an attack after all!

The greatest danger, and we must watch for it, is someone who withdraws only to attack again but from a safer distance. For them to try again to deal with it when we aren't around creates a genuine problem.

While the victorious Christian soldier engages the enemy on the line, he watches for the weaker who have straggled behind the lines. The responsible Christian leader is keeping an eye open for those who might otherwise straggle behind the grace of God.

I cannot define the grace of God any more than I can prove the existence of God. But I have experienced both and can try to describe them.

An example of grace would be a lady who is not being credited just for her clean house, good cooking, and polite words, but for certain other undefinable qualities. We ask, "How does she do it?"

No one has the answer—not even the gracious hostess. The best she can come up with, "I don't know; it's just me, I guess." That is a very good answer. It doesn't sound rational, but it seems right. Grace is not as much *what a person does* as *who he is*.

How does God do it? He's God. He made both cause and effect, and he can switch them around anyway he wishes and always come out right. There is no way God can do that and get this. But he does.

If God's grace is wonderful and amazing, it is astounding when it operates within the life of a believer. The grace of God enables a child of God to do something and get a result when there is no way in the world that a certain end can result from it. But it does.

THE GRACE OF GOD ENABLES A PERSON

to succeed without ability
and create without talent;

to be confident in doubt
and secure in turmoil;

to have joy in sorrow
and peace in battle;

to be loved without a lover
and helped without a helper;

to be healed without a physician
and taught without a teacher;

to be nourished without food
and assuaged without water;

to believe when doubtful
and trust when suspicious;

to love when hated
and care when rejected;

to see in the dark
and hear in the din;

to walk straight on a crooked path
and firmly on shifting sand;

to be sweet when bitterly assailed
and peaceful when hostilely attacked;

to make judgments sounder than my understanding
and decisions wiser than my knowledge.

The grace of God is
God acting in me
in spite of me.

"The root of bitterness," is a strange expression. Along with straggling behind the grace of God and becoming immoral or profane, the presence of a root of bitterness is part of falling apart. The root of bitterness must be rooted out and sweet fruit of the Spirit grown.

The metaphor appears earlier in the Scriptures. Moses wrote:

> Make sure there is no man or woman, clan or tribe among you today whose heart turns away from the Lord our God to go and worship the gods of those nations; make sure there is no root among you that produces such bitter poison (Deut. 29:18).

Those Hebrews fell behind in the wilderness and dropped out. Before they dropped out entirely, they poisoned the minds and spirits of the rest. After they were gone, their evil influence kept cropping up when least expected.

This root is bitter. It is the foul taste that remains in the mouth after the bad food has been spit out.

This bitterness is a root. The plant had been confidently chopped off at ground level. While the man is no longer watching carefully, it begins to grow again from the root that was left beneath the surface. It is fast growing, but the springing up is at least as much the result of careless inattention.

Simon Magus of Samaria was quite properly impressed with Peter's ability to impart the Holy Spirit by the laying on of hands. It was not Peter's ability, actually. That was Magus' assumption. Rather, it was God's sovereign choice to act through the instrumentality of that apostle. The converted sorcerer missed entirely Peter's concern to accomplish something for the people. Simon Magus was fascinated by the prospect of commercial exploitation. His conversion was not complete. There remained in him a root of the old, ungodly magic. It took only this occasion to make it an outcropping.

Peter exercised the necessary insight: "Your heart is not right before God. . . . For I see that you are full of bitterness and captive to sin" (Acts 8:21-23).

The root of bitterness is the perspective, values, and motives of sin cropping up into the Christian's life. It may still be rooted in the old life and spring up into the new. It may have spread from the evil world around.

It isn't enough to chop it off. It must be rooted out.

Have you ever attempted to pick asparagus out of a garden and plant another crop in its place? You don't just pick asparagus or you'll keep harvesting crop after crop of asparagus. You must dig deep and remove the entire plant, especially the root. Asparagus must be rooted out. Nothing less works.

We must examine everything we find in our minds and hearts. We must discriminate between what is there by the grace of God and what by the curse of sin.

When we borrow from the world, we must first judge what is planted in the world by the common grace of God and what is sown there as a product of sin. We fulfil God's creation when we cultivate the former, and we extend his redemption when we root out the latter. The procedure for such examination is, first, objective and then subjective.

We first concern ourselves to become thoroughly familiar with the teaching of Scripture about sin and righteousness. We take seriously the doctrine about living the biblical teaching of our spiritual elders. This much is relatively objective. What the Bible says it said well before we became involved, and it is objective to our special pleading.

Bible doctrine, which is based on the conceptions of man, does not enjoy the total and absolute objectivity of Scripture. Doctrine itself is not inspired. But we must consider with respect the convictions of those whose lives have demonstrated the validity of their doctrinal understanding.

Also, when the doctrine is common to spiritual leaders of distant places and separate times, it should take strong conviction and great knowledge for me to claim they were wrong and that I am right.

I also need to learn subjectively what the Holy Spirit thinks of my behavior. He will tell me whether the things in my life are from God or from the world. The Spirit of God will apply the Word of God to my life. And he will make specific application of biblical doctrine to those particulars that cannot be covered by a document as general and broad as the Bible.

Objective examination comes by way of Scripture. Subjective

examination comes by the Holy Spirit. By the two, we root out all roots of bitterness from elsewhere.

The root of bitterness has a corporate nature. It may begin with an individual, but it spreads throughout the body. Its very nature sometimes grows to epidemic dimensions. It sullies, infects, pollutes, diseases, corrupts, and destroys.

The spiritual leader's responsibility is to oversee the body so that no root of bitterness springs up. As well as looking to his own life, the leader watches over the lives of the group. He will allow nothing to defile the body.

Esau was infamous to the Hebrews since his disgraceful act had always been judged as the primary example of weakness of character and cheapness of behavior. The writer of Hebrews described him as being like one who is sexually immoral or godless (fornicator or profane). Never having been told Esau specifically practiced sexual immorality, the writer said something monstrously worse about him. The Greek word used identified a male prostitute, one who sells himself cheaply and loses himself in the process. He exchanges everything of value he has, and what little he gets is worth nothing at all.

No recovery is possible of what was lost. A lost thing can be found and returned. What is lost as described in this context is not a thing but part of the person. In fact, it *is* the person. He surrenders his personhood, and no person remains to recover anything. One may as well cut out his heart, give it away, and then expect to get it back and resume life.

In Esau's case, the thing of value was his birthright, the unique rights of the first-born. The first-born of Isaac, the son of Abraham, would normally have been the inheritor and transmitter of all the promises God made to Abraham. The term birthright was so culturally loaded that few twentieth century westerners are likely to understand its full meaning. Suffice it to say that Esau surrendered something truly precious. He gave up his uniqueness.

The metaphor's suggestion of sexually immoral is confirmed by the specific verb employed. It means to surrender, and the context suggests "to prostitute."

When one gives up his uniqueness for a non-thing, he has prostituted himself. Whatever is left is nothing of what it once was and could always have been.

It was lost, beyond redemption. "Afterward, as you know, when he wanted to inherit the blessing, he was rejected. He could bring about no change of mind, though he sought the blessing with tears" (v. 17).

When the Christian gives up finally his unique experience, redemption is unrelated to this specific loss. He is of all men most miserable. One who has salvation only as a possession and no longer an experience is no longer experiencing salvation and never again on this earth will live his life as a saving life.

However eternal—by the promise of God's grace—his life is, it enjoys no present reality. Because he refused to build up, he helplessly fell apart.

How, then, do we describe what is left—dropped in the wilderness of this world.

"Profane" did it quite well in 1611 when the Anglican heavy liturgy displayed what it means to be ecclesiastically profane or common. The monarchy and social class structure also demonstrated what it means to be a commoner, beneath royalty and peerage.

"Irreligious" is a short-sighted attempt, but "godless" a good try. The root word indicates the threshold of a building—that one architectural device upon which anyone could trample. Every house has a threshold, and every passerby could step all over it.

When applied to other things, it came to mean accessible to everyone without qualification, discrimination, or restraint. It was like the cheap, gaudy clothing sold in St. Audrey's market in Norwich, giving rise to *tawdry*. It was *sleazy* in the word's proper sense of flimsy or thin in texture or substance.

The late Senator Paul H. Douglas used to narrate the incredible exploits of one of Chicago's more notorious political bosses, Michael Kenna (1890-1940). Known with more fear than affection as "Hinky Dink," Senator Douglas concluded, " 'The Hink' knew the price of everything and the value of nothing."

For Esau and all truly profane persons, everything has its price, and nothing has any value.

The Christian who has prostituted himself has fallen apart to nothing better than the trash common to all the world's sewers. Esau would have later given everything he had and done everything he was able to regain what he sold out. But there could be no repentance. Without repentance, there could have been no forgiveness. Forgiveness being unavailable, so was redemption and restoration.

Machines deteriorate unless overhauled, and bodies degenerate unless rehabilitated. Spirits subside if they are not renewed. Machines, bodies, and spirits all need to be rebuilt. If they aren't, they will fall apart.

Sometimes breakdown results quite simply from being unused. Other times abuse is the cause. When the last remaining original part of a machine has been replaced by overhaul, we must acknowledge a different machine since there is no organic continuity. Although marvelous surgical repair and increasingly successful organ transplants have extended the life of bodies, the end comes as definitely as it ever has.

Machines and bodies have natural ends, and there is nothing to be done when they have reached that stage. Machines are scrapped without honor. Bodies are buried with somewhat more dignity. Not so with the spirit of a child of God. It lives on, and better, after the death of the body.

But what of the life of the spirit in this life? According to the warnings in the Epistle to the Hebrews, there can be a final breakdown in spiritual living. It can fall in the wilderness of its rebellion and not be allowed to enter into the promises it has refused to enter. The spirit, though still alive by the grace of God, no longer lives spiritually.

It has fallen apart, and there is no rebuilding. Not to be scrapped, it rusts in rejection. Not to be buried, it rots in disgrace.

However also according to the Epistle to the Hebrews, it does not need to be that way. It must not. We can build up. As long as it is today.

Man's spirit, which is closest to God of all he has created, need not sustain a final breakdown. No facility is inadequate for any task assigned by its Creator and Lord.

There is no limit to what a believer's spirit can become or accomplish. Any weakness, any failing can be rebuilt. But it must be, and promptly. The challenge of Hebrews is rebuild spiritual strength, move by straight steps, press on, build up.

SEVEN
PRESS ON

Whenever we conclude a Bible reading, we bring ourselves to a starting point. Scripture study should lead into biblical living. When we arrive at an understanding of the Bible, we go on to living its doctrine. This is the point of the warnings and exhortations.

HAVING BEEN UNDERSTOOD, STRIVE TO BE LIVING
Hebrews 4:12, 13

We understand the Bible only with the recognition that it understands us. It knows our lives, what they have been, what they are now, and what they can become.

Most people begin reading the Bible objectively and passively, as some literary object that they pick up and open. The more secular people read it as they would most pieces of good literature. They try to understand it, perhaps even to master it. The more religious read it as one approaches a holy thing. They try to reverence it, perhaps even to worship it.

Either way, it is an object they read only passively. They aren't part of what they read, and it isn't part of them.

Should we give the Bible as much as a decent reading from a human standpoint, something likely happens to us. When we read it as Scripture, almost certainly it impacts upon us. The Bible is the Word of God, and the Word of God is active and effective. The Scripture discerns us spiritually more sharply than a two-edged sword cuts us physically.

Nothing is hidden before the Word of God; it understand us. It acts upon us, and it has its intended effect upon us.

As this occurs, we begin to read the Bible subjectively and actively. We read it to find ourselves as its subject and actively enter into its story. The Bible changes lives as it admits us to what God has promised.

The Epistle to the Hebrews warns Christian believers because it knows the danger most people have as a result of carelessness. The writer understood that we need to be warned or we would continue into the danger toward which we are already heading by indifferently or purposely rejecting the facts.

The Epistle to the Hebrews exhorts Christian believers because it knows the potential all enjoy as a result of God's promise. The epistle encourages us so we won't hold back from the promises from which we are now shrinking. The writer understood the need of those who were foolishly timid or irresponsibly resisting the promise.

The writer (whoever he was) personally understood the first century readers (whoever they were), and he must have embarrassed them by what he both knew and understood. He encouraged them the same way. He understood them, and they must have responded to his understanding.

His letter became included in the canon of Scripture. As the Word of God, the Epistle to the Hebrews (and to us) understands today's readers. It embarrasses us by what it says, and it can so encourage us. Since it explains us so well, we must respond to its understanding.

The experience of being understood by Scripture impresses the responsive person deeply. One of my seminary students described his experience as we fellowshiped under the tall pines at the Glendawn Bible Conference on the shores of Washington's Puget Sound. He had been listening to me preach through the epistle, and my exposition brought to mind previous experience with the warnings and exhortations.

He was a very satisfied Christian, content with himself and his religious status. Reared in the church, he had accepted Christ and was baptized, learned the Sunday school lessons, and recently had been elected a junior deacon. People in his church were satisfied with him. He was teaching Sunday school without taking it seriously or working at it. One of the lessons he taught was the part we had gone over that night.

He recalled, "As I read in my little New Testament, I sensed something distantly familiar. Assuming I had read this before, I tried to shake it off. Then I began to feel a little pressure, a cold, clammy feeling. Then I felt a rather spinning sensation, as if I had been lifted out of myself and now was looking down upon myself, reading the Bible, like those visions in *A Christmas Carol*. At the same time, I felt in the middle of things with everyone looking at me. I actually looked around to see, but could see nothing. Yet, I couldn't escape the feeling. Someone— or something—was watching me.

"I put the thoughts from my mind and forced myself to read on. I had to get this done. But it got worse. I had been here before—someone was watching. Someone was, in fact, talking to me. Not the same time I was reading, but in the reading. No, from the reading. The Bible was actually talking to me—about me. It is the story of my life, neglecting my salvation—hardening my heart—not believing—disobeying—not being sorry—falling along the wayside—sinning on purpose. It's all there, all of it. The Bible knows. It knows me, and now I'm beginning to catch on."

Indeed, he was excited! His life demonstrates the power of the Word of God better by far than my words could ever describe it.

"The Word of God is living and active" (4:12). In its peculiar function, the Word of God discriminates between elements otherwise seen as indivisible. A person may be able to pass an offense off as simple and unadulterated, but not past the Word of God.

The Word of God is dynamic and effective in judging man, both his being and behavior. It explains what man ought to be and what he is. It shows, in theory, what man ought to do and what he does.

When a Christian believer comes to the place of God's rest, God's Word makes a judgment. If he be qualified to enter, the Word gives entrance. If he be unqualified, the Word denies entrance.

The warnings can prepare man for this judgment. And so can the exhortations. If they humble us by their insightful assessment, they humiliate us by final judgment.

The Word of God knows us in our being—both immaterial being ("soul and spirit") and material being ("joints and marrow").

I've long been amused at how silly some patients can be in resisting the judgment of their physicians. "It's my body!" they say. But the doctor knows more about their bodies than they do. Such people have a good deal more basis to resist a psychologist's diagnosis of their minds. But not against the Word of God! It can see the soul as distinct from the spirit as it can the joints from the marrow.

The Word of God exposes us in our behavior—both emotional ("thoughts") and intellectual ("intentions"). It divides the thoughts and intentions "of the heart," the real person.

We can successfully act out happiness before other people or put on the act of sadness with equal success. We can convince examiners that we believe the doctrine of faith or that we do not believe in a sinful practice.

Lest we understand this amazing knowledge to be restricted to humans, the writer stated that: "Nothing in all creation is hidden from God's sight. Everything is uncovered and laid bare before the eyes of him to whom we must give account" (Heb. 4:13).

The Bible is the living, active Word of God. When we open the Bible to ourselves, the Bible opens us to ourselves. The book that understands us helps us to understand who we should be and what we are.

The Word of God is the Bible, to be sure. But the Bible is the Word of God because it is the expression of the Son of God, who himself is the Word of God.

Jesus the Christ, during his days as the Word-become-flesh, understood people and revealed what was in people so that they came to know themselves as Christ had always known them. While Matthew, Mark, and Luke narrate this revealing Word, it was the Apostle John who explained it.

At the very beginning of time and space, John wrote, this Word not only was with God but was God himself. In him was life, and this life was the light of all men. Although this light shines in the darkness of evil, that darkness has never been able to extinguish it. Although the actual maker of the world was really in the world, the world didn't know him. But he knew men because the Word became incarnate—the Word of God became flesh and lived for a while in the very midst of men. Yet, he remained the Word of God, full of grace and truth (John 1:1-14).

Jesus so precisely identified Nathanael's activity and so accurately described his character, he astounded the new disciple who could but wonder, "How do you know me?" (John 1:48). The Lord not only knew that this "true Israelite" searched, he revealed the One for whom he searched.

Although many Jerusalem people believed in Jesus' name because of his signs, he didn't entrust himself to them because he knew all men without any information from any of them. He, himself, knew what was in man (John 2:24, 25).

In Samaria, Jesus knew of food unknown to his disciples who searched for it, and of water that the woman missed. After attracting her attention through pointing out some sensitive facts about her life, he revealed the real meaning of her life. She told neighbors to come and see a man who told her all she ever did. Her word was impressive, but his person became persuasive once they experienced him (4:1-42). The Lord knew all about them and what they did, and he revealed to them why they did it.

The question to Philip about feeding the crowd was only a test because he himself knew what he would do and, afterward, he knew what the crowd would do so that he could protect himself from what he knew about them. He knew from the very first not only those who would believe in him but also the one who should betray him (6:6-64).

The Jews marveled that Jesus should possess learning when he had never studied (7:15). Some of the elders thought to inform on an adulterous woman, only to be shocked at what he knew of their private lives and crushed by what he let them see of themselves so that they walked away in speechless disgrace (7:59—8:11). Since he is the light of the world, on the other hand, those who follow him do not walk in such darkness but have the light of life (8:12). This self-confident knowledge of secret things upset the Pharisees. But Jesus explained to them, "I judge with the judgment of the Father" (8:16).

How does the good shepherd so unfailingly lead and feed his sheep? Simple, he said. I know my own (10:14). On and on we could go in the Gospel of John.

This Jesus, the Word of God become man, was who the Bible was all about. People who, years ago, listened to the Living Word came to know themselves. We, today, who read the written Word come to know ourselves. As we accept and trust the Word, we are enlightened about life and come to understand ourselves.

Jesus became the man that every man was supposed to be but that no man ever was. In seeing him, we see what we should be. As it is, however, we do not see ourselves as such. But we do see Jesus, who became like us in order to become the priest who helps us become a man in the Man for all men. Referring to Psalm 8, the writer to the Hebrews explained this reciprocal identification in relation to the first warning and the first exhortation (2:5-18).

Because of what the Word of God knows and tells us about ourselves, "Let us therefore make every effort to enter that rest . . . the Word of God is living and active" (4:11, 12).

A student works harder at study when he finds a teacher who understands his problems and helps him. He strives to graduate so that he doesn't drop out by the same sort of disobedience that was the downfall of former students. Those just attended classes without learning until, finally, they dropped out.

Let us work harder at living since we have found the Teacher, and his text, who understands us and is here to help. Let us strive to enter into the rest God promised to us so that we don't drop out by the same sort of disobedience that was the downfall of the former Hebrews. They went in circles in the wilderness without recovering until, finally, they dropped in the wilderness without ever entering into the land that had been promised.

Strive, then, with what? All that the Bible reveals to us, especially about ourselves. When we realize the warnings understand us, we turn to the exhortations because they also understand us.

HAVING BEEN WARNED AND EXHORTED, LIVE Hebrews 2:1—12:17

The warnings in this epistle were intended to be taken with seriousness. Equally important is the need to take them in balance with the exhortations and in proportion to the total message of the book. If people take them lightly, they miss the unique contribution of this epistle, so crucial to the central teachings of the New Testament. If people neurotically distort the warnings, they destroy themselves and lose all hope for wholesomeness and victory in life.

Perhaps no other book in the Bible suffers more distortions as well as dilutions than Hebrews. Because some claim the doctrine of eternal security so firmly, they refuse to consider what the warnings of Hebrews do mean, even just in their own contexts. Once dismissed, the warnings are conveniently forgotten. Such thoughtless people surrender the epistle's value for themselves and reject it as the Word of God.

So, too, some think those troublesome passages intended for the unsaved. Those who believe this will accept everything in the epistle—except the warnings, which they refuse to believe have anything to do with their own salvation. So they refuse to do anything themselves with their salvation.

The first principle to observe in reading the warning passages is to read what is there in its own right without either reading something foreign into it or worrying about what it might lead to. We must not try to read between the lines or say "in other words" and then construct upon the statement a doctrine that quite thoroughly contradicts the text.

When we read, "How shall we escape if we neglect such a great salvation?" (2:3), we must not insert "hell" after "neglect."

When we read, "They were not able to enter, because of their unbelief" (3:19) we must not take it with the recognition that "his rest" (v. 18) is the reference. We shouldn't insert "heaven" by misconstruing the geographical figures of the epistle's wilderness motif.

So, too, when we read, "Let us fear lest any of you be judged to have failed to reach it" (4:1, RSV). We need to take the subordinate clause with which the same sentence begins, which makes clear that it is "entering his rest." It is not ours to change this, either.

When we read, "For it is impossible to restore again to repentance" (6:4, RSV), we must take literally the plain word "repentance," and not substitute anything else, such as "salvation" or "eternal life." Nor may we modify "impossible" with something like "almost."

When we read: "For if we sin deliberately after receiving the knowledge of the truth, there no longer remains a sacrifice for sins" (10:26, RSV), we must not take it that Christ's sacrifice isn't sufficient for repented sins. It simply does not say that.

The warning statements are generally difficult, to be sure. Yet they are reasonably clear explanations of complex human experience. When they are seen in light of cosmic reality, they can be understood, and we can use them well. The basic requirement for understanding is a willingness to understand what is meant, and a willingness to do what is directed.

I suppose I worry the more, however, about a more common purpose in distortion—and it's weird. Some people know very well what they intend. They interpret the warnings into such monstrous distortions there is no way anyone is going to take them seriously.

Some people, however, distort these warnings purposely. They appear determined to rid themselves of unacceptable parts of the teaching. Their method is to twist the statements so they appear to say something that doesn't pertain to a child of God to whom the Father has promised eternal life. If they can only succeed in reassigning at least these disturbing passages to people of another status, they can go their merry way. I realize that my suspicions come not as much from examination of their doctrinal statements as they do from observation of human behavior.

Dilutions and distortions of this epistle's teachings, especially the warnings, are tragically common. Let's not do either. Let's take the warnings seriously and reasonably so we understand them wholesomely and use them productively. So, too, let's take the exhortations seriously.

Sometimes the writer of Hebrews used the imperative mood (giving a command) of the verb and in the second person plural, "You people do this." This is then, in grammar, a command for others to take action rather than an invitation to join the writer in the action.

However, the characteristic commands of the Bible are given by persons who are themselves already engaged in the action commanded of others. Think of the commands from Moses, Samuel, the prophets, Jesus, and all the apostles to their followers. "Do as I am already doing" is the equivalent of "Let us together do this."

I point this out because some of the statements in Hebrews that are regularly termed exhortations are really imperatives. The language context of the statements and, especially, the spirit of the writer yields them encouragements.

Some actual exhortations by language are often translated by various versions, commentaries, and preachers as imperatives. So it is, "Lay hold," "Do it," "Go on," "Draw near," "Build up." All are imperative statements that render exhortations, as they seem to have greater impact in this form.

But the biblical writers and all caring persons who present the Bible are willing to include themselves in the imperative by putting it as an exhortation, saying, in effect, "We are in this together."

Preachers typically introduce a challenge by their testimony of the experience. Says one, "I am trying to do this. Join me in this experience." Then as he leaves the hearer with the message from Scripture, the final challenge is, "Do it."

However much the preacher must himself listen, preaching is designed as the occasion for the listener to respond to the preacher who knows enough and cares enough to address the hearer by sharing his convictions and concerns.

In listening to a preacher say, "We *all* have this need," we dare not take it that we can ignore that he is talking to us, too. Despite how many others must also respond, we must respond as if we were the only people with the responsibility.

If the race is worth running, it is worth running even if we are left to go it alone. The excitement of the crowd running with us can carry us to the starting line, but the pack soon thins out. Then we find it easier to fall behind since fewer remain to encourage us. With fewer companions and the leaders ahead out of sight, we find ourselves dropping out of the race entirely.

If we are not comfortable going to the starting line alone, we might never reach the finish line since that could also require a solo performance.

When exhortations are given, we must listen to them as if others are in it with us, but we must obey the imperatives as if they were our own immediate responsibilities.

The visitation chairman announces to your congregation, "We need at least ten people to volunteer for calling at the homes of new residents. Who will be first to volunteer?"

That first is the hardest to get. Why not be the first to step forward in response? Why wait for others? Wouldn't it be that much easier to call with the reassurance that we freely chose to perform this ministry without having to be dragged into it by those ahead of us? And wouldn't it satisfy to realize we had achieved leadership simply by seizing an individual opportunity, even if it might have meant going it alone?

Many times a group of people have worked together on a project although the group was a long time in forming. Weeks may have elapsed before the first person responded. The next two people came the following week. After that, it was a steady flow of joiners. Almost every worthy group started with a loner willing to do it alone, if that's what it should take. But the task didn't, because one person finally took it upon himself, and others followed.

Two people avoid each other because both are angry at what each did to the other. Who should be first to come back? The elder? The man? The leader? No matter. When offense has occurred, the first to apologize ought to be the one who first recognizes the offense.

It is inaccurate for a third party to say, "Let 'us' make up." One of the aggrieved persons needs to say to the other, "Let *us* make up." That's the time for exhortation. The third party should be able to say, "Make up, you two." The two then should try to be first with, "Let's make up."

When confronted by the right thing to do, we should do it without fussing about whether it be an exhortation or imperative. Exhortations may seem nicer, but imperatives may be more to the point.

The writer's five formal exhortations serve a function.

This first was "Let us be alert" (2:1-4). Lay hold, lest you drift away. "We must pay more careful attention, therefore, to what we have heard" (v. 1).

Secondly, "Let us be careful" (3:7—4:13). Do it, lest you disbelieve. "There remains, then, a Sabbath-rest for the people of God; for anyone who enters God's rest also rests from his own work, just as God did from his. Let us, therefore, make every effort to enter that rest" (4:9-11). Let us live spiritual lives and take God's promises.

These lead to the third exhortation, "Let us go on" (5:11—

6:20). Go on, lest you fall back. "Therefore let us leave the elementary teachings about Christ and go on to maturity" (6:1). Let us go on in spiritual growth.

The fourth, "Let us draw near" (10:19-39). Draw near, lest you walk away. "Let us draw near to God with a sincere heart in full assurance of faith. . . . Let us hold unswervingly to the hope we profess. . . . And let us consider how we may spur one another on" (vv. 22-24). Choose to become intimate with God.

And the fifth exhortation, "Let us build up" (12:12-17). Build up, lest you fall apart. "Therefore, strengthen your feeble arms and weak knees. Make level paths for your feet. . . . Make every effort to live. . . . See to it that. . . ." (vv. 12-15). Build up to top spiritual condition by conditioning yourself spiritually.

The writer gave other exhortations, and we shall yet consider one of them which is something of a capstone (12:1-3) and close with the word about exhortations (13:22).

The writer confronted his readers with a warning (negative) and challenges them with an exhortation (positive). This seems to balance his appeal as well as being comprehensive of the scope of people's needs.

These expressions, all using the word "lest," were crafted for the sake of this book in order to create neatly packaged case points and chapter titles. But they come honestly because all of them are clearly implied within the text, and the idea flavors all the writer said about spiritual responsibility.

The "lests" are easily recognized in the language. They take either of two forms, one an idiom, literally translated "in order that not" and the other means literally either "not when" or "not at all."

In the King James Version, both expressions are almost always translated as "lest." Modern versions more frequently favor something like "so that not." While this reflects contemporary English, "lest" is a convenient, if old-fashioned, term because it clearly identifies the grammar by its consistency.

English dictionaries identify *lest* as a conjunction with the sense of "for fear that." Do it, for fear that you should otherwise disbelieve.

The "for fear that" statements begin with a verb expressing positive purpose. These are either exhortations or imperatives that have the force of encouragements. The positive purpose, the action desired, is connected by the "lest" to a negative purpose clause, the undesirable consequences if the positive purpose should fail.

Greek writers expressed the negative verb in a tense and a mood that make it a strong prohibition. The tense used, the aorist tense, doesn't exist in English. In Greek it indicates that a point in time has no part in the reference. A negative verb so put means this thing should never, ever happen—not past, nor present, nor future.

The mood, often unrecognized in English, is the subjunctive that expresses a provisional situation. It could be put "Draw near, that at no time should you walk away."

All this is to say that escaping a condition about which we are warned is not nearly enough. If we don't then go on to accomplish another experience to which we are also exhorted, we get hit from another direction. Such is identified by the conjunction "lest."

We are warned, in the first warning statement, not to neglect using our salvation. And, in turn, the first exhortation encourages us to lay hold. As part of the very statement of exhortation, however, is the "lest." "We must pay more careful attention to what we have heard" (the exhortation) "lest we drift away from it."

This is the regular pattern, "Be warned. Let's be encouraged, lest you should. . . ."

Text	Positive Purpose	Lest	Negative Purpose
2:1	We must pay more careful attention, therefore, to what we have heard	lest	we should drift away.
3:12	Be careful	lest	there should be in any of you an evil, unbelieving heart.
4:1	Let us be careful	lest	any of you should be found to have fallen short.

4:11	Let us, therefore, make every effort to enter that rest	lest	anyone should fall
12:3	Consider him who persisted ...	lest	you should grow weary or lose heart.
12:12, 13	Strengthen your feeble arms and weak knees. Make level paths for your feet	lest	the lame should be disabled.

Closely related to these are still other variations of the expressions. One of them is put in wish form. "We want (desire that) each of you to show the same diligence to the very end, in order to make your hope sure. We do not want you to become lazy but to imitate those who ... inherit what has been promised" (6:11, 12). Such statements force the same response as did the long list of qualities which the Apostle Paul prayed to be enjoyed by his readers. The apostles' very wish, for their disciples, became a command.

Another is an additional purpose that accompanies an exhortation: "Make every effort to live in peace ... and to be holy" (12:14). "See to it that no one misses the grace of God and that no bitter root grows up to cause trouble" (v. 15); "... that no one is sexually immoral" (v. 16).

These warnings and exhortations can be expressed by three English verbs, which describe specific actions of the strong and growing Christian. The sins about which the writer warned, the serious believer will *exclude* from his life. The righteous behaviors toward which he exhorts, that kind of person will *include* in his life. The evil consequences he indicates, the growing Christian will *preclude* from his life.

We grab hold of sins and throw them out. We lay hold of righteous acts and fix them within. We never touch, or as much as go near, the evil consequences of ignoring the warnings and neglecting the exhortations.

To preclude sin by staying away from it seems to be harder to understand than either excluding sin or including righteousness, even though it is perhaps the easiest of the three actions to take.

It is hard to accept the warnings, since to do so we are admitting a dangerous trend in our behavior. It is easier to respond to the exhortations because we are built to do those things. It is easier to smile than to frown, for example.

If you have heeded the warning and are concentrating on the exhortation, you need not worry about the consequences. You won't drift away from the realities you have been taught if you lay hold of those realities.

Drifting away and disbelieving and falling back and walking away and falling apart are all precluded by laying hold and doing it and going on and drawing near and building up.

The secret of spiritual victory is not an esoteric manipulation of a reluctant god. Nor is it the moral triumph of a superman. The genius of the normal Christian life is believing obedience to a loving and caring Lord. You will preclude disobedient sinning by including obedient righteousness.

One of the hardest lessons for children and youth to learn—but a crucial one—is to do what they are taught by faithful parents lest they fall into plights for which they did not need to be prepared. Children would not need to be taught not to get into fights if they would play with peaceful friends rather than tangle with fighting strangers.

Some Christian teenagers hang around hangouts and then wonder how they got into trouble. The simple answer, so often necessary, is "You shouldn't have been there in the first place. If you had been where you should have been, that would never have happened."

Unfortunately more than a few Christian parents, wise enough to come up with such advice, are also foolish enough to forget the lesson when they confront the more subtle dangers themselves. They, too, fall into sin because they fail to preclude sin by practicing righteousness.

How does a husband remain faithful to his wife, for instance? He precludes unfaithfulness by acting faithfully toward his trusting wife. He practices his love for her, to her. He does not try romantic affection on another woman. Flirting, or fooling around, or whatever euphemism is employed, simply has no place in the life of a faithful husband or a faithful wife. A husband must not act as a lover to another woman. A wife must not allow another man to be a lover to her, not even jokingly or playfully. Nor may they experiment or fantasize. They must not even think about it. When the thought approaches—and it will—they must immediately reject it. If it enters, they must promptly expel it from the mind. Such thoughts are best precluded by thinking in different ways and directions, so that the harmful thoughts aren't there to stumble upon.

Let's use this principle throughout our lives and in every regard. As we respond to the exhortations in Hebrews, and those elsewhere in Scripture, and in the encouraging ministries God sends to you from brothers, we will do the right, and preclude the wrong.

In understanding the language of the Epistle to the Hebrews, then, we should watch for "lest" and "so that."

If the writer's exhortation has produced in our lives, we have precluded the evil consequences. If the encouragement begins to wear off, we must recall the kicker that always follows hard onto it:

Press on, lest you should fall behind and then drop out. All the warnings and "lests" notwithstanding, God's saving gift of eternal life is secure both by God's promise and his person.

If the biblical term "eternal life" should not indicate spiritual life to be eternal, the term would have no meaning and the gift, no value. But it does, because the gift with which God endows those who accept it is nothing less than the eternal life of his own Son, who is one with the Father. No theological stipulation is required because there can be no stronger evidence of the eternal security of our salvation than the definition God gave to it: eternal.

Salvation is, by God's definition, eternally secure.

The Christian believer must capitalize on the doctrine of eternal security for assurance, but not exploit it and become careless. It should make him confident, but not presumptuous.

Careless and presumptuous is just what the Hebrews were. So the writer restrained his observations about eternal security and concentrated on that sense in which one can lose salvation. An eternally saved believer can fail to repent of newly committed sin and thereby lose the experience of salvation. Failing to preclude possible sin, even if eventually forgiven, is a salvation loss.

If these failures degenerate into refusal and failing to appropriate salvation from sins becomes the course of one's life, that person merely holds salvation as a static possession but has lost it as a continuing experience. His heart has become hardened, and there is no entering to the promise.

Hebrews, as we said earlier, teaches us to live actively a saving life, to be increasingly free of sin. Some will wonder if to do so indulges a doctrine of sinless perfection. No. None of that!

Sinless perfection is a meaningless term because it is an impossible condition. It cannot become true for us until God calls us into his holy presence or Christ returns to earth in final redemption.

It is interesting that the same people who presume upon the doctrine of eternal security are so contemptuous of those who believe the doctrine of sinless perfection. It sounds as if they are challenging the arrogance of the claimants. In fact, they have found one more excuse for not living their own salvation.

That we cannot now be entirely free from all sin is theologically sound. But that is not the point. The Bible challenges us to be increasingly free from all sin, which *is* possible.

Being increasingly free of sin, even without reaching sinlessness or absolute perfection, makes it possible for today's believer to enter into the realm of all that God has promised. Those blessings we read about in the Bible that we understand are, for the most part, not heavenly blessings but earthly. Many of the goals we may have thought must await heaven are available here and now.

In fact, any earthly blessing missed on earth is missed for eternity. Live life, as God has told us to live it, to its fullest—this is our only chance.

Placing a high value on physical life and our earthly mission does not in the slightest detract from heaven or take from its better things. Hebrews would have us honor God's creation and exercise stewardship for it.

Remember that the action verb is "entering" not "having entered." "Entering in" to God's promises is a continuing experience rather than a final accomplishment. The task is to be entering, not to think we can have entered. We must always be in the process of maturing since we cannot reach final maturity here on earth.

Remember, too, the nature and purpose of religion. Remember also that experience is the goal. Religion is a system of mechanical devices used as a vehicle toward spiritual experience. Be cautious about the vehicle. Demand the real thing, and be as religious as necessary and as spiritual as possible.

LIVE LIFE, AND YOU WILL ACCOMPLISH LIFE Hebrews 12:1-3

The strong word *persistence* describes the active life. Let us *persist.* Life is not so much ended as it is accomplished. Life, by its very nature, is success. These concepts need to engage us because they, too, present encouragement for discouraged Christians.

I like to paraphrase this very challenging passage:

> Let us run with *persistence* the race that is set before us. Let us fix our eyes on Jesus . . . who for the joy that was set before him *persisted* in the cross. . . . Consider him who *persisted* against such opposition . . . so that you will not grow weary or lose heart (12:1-3).

Patience is, surely, part of the effort needed to run life as one runs a race. One does well to exercise an active patience. Yet, this English attempt fails to convey the sense of the writer's word, and also seriously misses the force of his metaphor.

I have already mentioned that this word and its related forms are regularly translated "persistence" (noun) and "persist" (verb). In some contexts, "perseverance" might well be favored, and it makes good sense to encourage, "Let us run the race with perseverance" (NIV, RSV).

Yet we must choose between the two possibilities. *Persevere* nearly always implies an admirable quality and, so, fits here. *Persist,* more often suggests a disagreeable or annoying quality. If *patience* is too mild to describe the action of race running, then *perseverance* is too pleasant. Active living of life does accomplish decidedly pleasant things, and many of its steps are pleasureable. But the striving of living is often not pleasant.

Despite how the steps balance out on the pleasant-unpleasant scale when at last the race has been completed, it is most effectively run with first expectations of its unpleasantness. Otherwise, the pleasant steps will soften us and we will lose the persistence needed for the others. Better to expect the worst and be surprised by the occasional good than to count on the best and be demoralized by the worst.

Recall the worst case scenario God gave the prophet when he called him to ministry (Isaiah 6), which the evangelist of greatest perspective later applied to Jesus Christ as the story of his life (John 12). It is Jesus, the writer of Hebrews told us, on whom we are to fix our eyes in the race. Let's expect, then, what Jesus did.

The word *persist* usually stresses stubbornness or obstinacy more than courage or patience. In the kind of society in which we must live a life considered foreign, courageous stubbornness is precisely the requirement.

Finally, the word often implies opposition to advice or determination against opposition. While living life actively and running the race follows well the writer's exhortation, it goes very much against the most frequent advice given, such as "Go with the flow," "Do your own thing," "Cool it, man."

Against advice? It ignores advice and defies demands not only from the world, but sometimes from other Christians. "Stubborn" and "obstinate" describe the committed believer. Stubborn? Obstinate? Sure, why not?

And opposition. I'll tell you about opposition. In distance running, it's the name of the game. The weather is one thing to fight. The temperature can change from dehydrating highs to freezing lows. The wind causes hyperventilation and buffeting. The humidity can be debilitating and oppressive. The hills are arduous upward and hazardous downward. The surface can be dusty, muddy, boggy, slippery, or rough. The body feels pain, soreness, cramps, fatigue, strain, or stress. The mind becomes resistive and bored, or confused, or discouraged.

Running is against opposition.

I have never run a race with patience, and *perseverance* has never suggested itself. Persistence. That's it. I will not drop out. I will not fall back. I will persist—and keep persisting.

The Hebrew language offers an idiom that would please the writer of Hebrews: "Persisting, let us perish." Other versions use "endurance," "resolution," and "steadily." All good, but *persistence* seems better still.

The Apostle Paul agreed. "I beat my body and make it my slave" (1 Cor. 9:27).

Let us fix our eyes, in this race, on Jesus because he persisted in the experience of the cross. Yet, he thought not of the pain but of the joy. There was joy, but there just wasn't much happiness along the road to Calvary. He carried a joy within, which found itself in what was to be accomplished. And the nearer Jesus came to the cross and the more pain he felt, the more he spoke of joy.

Fixing our eyes upon Jesus in his persistence toward the cross requires not looking around at the relative performance of other people or looking down at our own subjective feelings. We must fix in our working minds the performance of the historical Jesus and reinforce the conviction that the eternal Christ now performs his work in our lives. To submit to weariness or to lose heart is not allowing Christ to do those greater things in us. We must let go of our feelings of failure, and fix upon the success of the indwelling Christ.

We tend to look at life too closely. We look so microscopically that what we see isn't life at all. It's something like being so fascinated by the trees we can't appreciate the forest. The advice and counsel we are getting about life fix our attention upon one or another component of life to the extent it degenerates into a fixation that misses the whole point of life. We suffer movements that turn cultish, and we endure language that scrambles to jargon.

Take parenting, for example. Fathers do not live as fathers, and mothers are not mothers. No longer are they individuals in relation to persons. The traditional relationships now are to be sophisticated into things one does to other social units. With the children deposited at a care center, parents spend weekends at motels in the city, feverishly filling in loose-leaf manuals from videotapes on parenting. Then they rush home late Sunday evening and practice techniques on the kids until the next seminar with the newest expert. They are "parenting?" No. They are *into* parenting, as they call it in the jargon of the day.

No wonder. It started with their being into "bonding," as they call it. They don't consider how they may get to know the kid when they change his diapers. But they are *into* bonding.

They are also *into* midlife crisis about the time they are into "burn-out." Everybody knows the symptoms and dutifully produces them. If it doesn't work, fake it.

About the time they weary of being *into* stress management, they get *into* death-and-dying. (The more academic get *into* thanatology.) Then they abandon a dying mother to silent death because it is all so mental. They understand everything, but can't feel anything. Their own death is announced, and they think they cope because they can name the stages of dying as they occur.

I'm being a little silly, I know. I believe in every one of these entirely worthwhile studies. But I believe in something far more important. I believe in living life actively and I believe in persistent living and I believe in accomplishing life.

Let's not pull threads from life's fabric and think we have whole cloth. Let's not extract functional components from the machine and expect to operate a functioning system. What life is about is not being "into" abstractions, but *being,* experiencing concrete reality.

When medical students dissect a human body, they put the heart there, a foot here, and the brain over there. The student looks at each in and of itself, isolated from its organic connection with the others. He learns a frightful amount about cardiology, orthopedics, and neurology. But since it is an academic exercise, he learns little about life and nothing about living.

The scientist knows no more about life by examining an organ than he creates life in a cadaver by putting pieces back together, even in anatomical order. Life in a body is more than the sum of the body parts. Life is infinitely greater than these.

So, too, with all of life. We can learn, if we apply carefully, much from the current wellness and holistic health perspectives. I commend the interests for physical health and recommend them for application to emotional and spiritual health.

We need balanced growth of the organic whole. Life is something like that, but a whole lot more.

Periodically, then, we need to step back from all these individual things and survey the wholeness of life. We need to determine if any of these things have subtracted from life and insure they add up to life.

Biblical descriptions of life as doctrine and the narratives of lives as they were really lived lay the foundation. Searching prayer will open our lives to the light of Scripture. The feedback of trustworthy, trusted brothers and sisters will redirect and reinforce our self-examination.

The final test, it seems to me, comes by considering the impact of our lives upon other lives. If my children, for instance, have not become better persons as a result of what I have done as a father, parenting remained a "thing" and I haven't been a father at all.

None of us will ever know all there is to know about life, and we can't ever expect to understand much of it. But we can all experience it, all of it. We experience life by living life, full life, the wholeness of life. With life so full and meaningful, one wonders how one could be happy to leave it.

When, in God's time, we leave earth, if, indeed, we have entered into the promise, there is a peculiar sorrow at leaving the good things and good times our gracious Lord has given his faithful children. That sorrow is not consistent, in terms of rational analysis, with the even greater joy of appearing within the immediate presence of our Lord. Yet, I think it is entirely appropriate for a fulfilled Christian believer to go kicking and screaming into heaven.

When that saint reaches heaven though, he'll be embarrassed by such sentiment. But he'll be greeted by the indulgent smile of the High Priest who understands because he's been there.

So earthly life ends. Sometimes it is terminated by others. Other times we just seem to run out of steam.

Not so, the writer said. Consider Joseph (11:22). "By faith Joseph, when his end was near, spoke." One could translate it, "Joseph, at the accomplishment of his life."

If you live life persistently, you will accomplish life. That's why God created us and the Son redeemed us—so we could live life that we accomplish life. That is successful spiritual living.

How does one succeed in life? The same way any substantial success is achieved. It begins with a decision. One decides to reject spiritual death or mere spiritual existence, and one decides to live. He chooses life. That kind of life is a choice.

Although a clear decision begins the move toward success, it must be followed firmly by another act, commitment. One must commit himself to the thing upon which he has decided. Decision is the start, and commitment is the follow-up. It accomplishes nothing to make a good decision, if we do not commit ourselves and act upon that commitment.

I decide to become prayerful, for instance. I must, then, dedicate time for prayer, leave other activities, engage myself in the act of praying, and refuse to be distracted from it. I must, finally, stay at praying until prayer is accomplished. My decision toward prayer became implemented by my commitment in praying. Only then do I pray successfully.

Decision + Commitment = Success. It always does. Nothing else will do it. If you live life persistently, you will accomplish life as a success.

TOLERATE THE EXHORTATION, AND PRESS ON Hebrews 13:22

One final word on exhortations. This epistle is "this word of exhortation" (13:22). The writer urged us to pay attention to this word since "I have written only a short letter." But it was long enough!

He articulated enough specific exhortations for us to have sufficient encouragement. The task remains to accept and respond.

The Greek word for *word* means "story," as in the "ology" which is the suffix on many English words for studies. Theology is the study of God, the word on God. Call this exhortology, if you will, but it is what we need to live life, to press on.

Modern versions improve the King James Bible's "suffer this word of exhortation" by translating it "I urge you to bear with this exhortation." Other contexts for the word suggest the sense of "tolerate." It also fits here. If your body is healthy, it will tolerate strong food. "Tolerate exhortation as a healthy body absorbs food and turns it into nourishment for self and energy for work," the writer was saying.

The writer didn't ask us to put up with what he says. He was burdened that we take in what he said, ingest it. We must turn it into spiritual strength and energy. We must build ourselves up, and work for others.

We must not resent those who warn, and not fight those who exhort.

We may put up with the warners and the exhorters, perhaps, but tolerate what they say when they do so biblically and when led by the Spirit. The Holy Spirit directed the writer of Hebrews to give them a word of exhortation. The Spirit led the Church to include this epistle in the canon of Scripture for us

"Hebrews." The same Spirit will lead people of the Word to us with this word of exhortation. We must tolerate the word.

The goal, of course, is not to subscribe to what I have written about the Word that is Scripture, but to tolerate the Word of Scripture and respond to the Spirit.

We have served encouragement to you. The ball is now in your court. Accept responsibility for your life, and live it.

Aside from the epistle's final greetings, you have the writer's final imperative:

"Brothers, I urge you to bear with my word of exhortation, for I have written you only a short letter."

Press on.

Books in the Living Studies Series:

Living Studies books are intended to be a simple, practical approach to Adult Sunday school electives. The carefully selected books for this series and the thought-provoking Leader's Guides that accompany each of the books provide an exciting way to retivalize your Bible study or Sunday school class. Leader's Guides are based on sound educational principles, designed to transform your class into an active participating discussion group.

BIBLE STUDIES

Colossians: A Portrait of Christ, Dr. James T. Draper, Jr. Verse-by-verse application of Bible truths that speak to today's issues. 13 sessions.

Discover Joy: Studies in Philippians, Dr. James T. Draper, Jr. Reasons why believers can face any circumstances of life or death with delight instead of despair. 13 sessions.

Faith That Works: Studies in James, Dr. James T. Draper, Jr. James wrote not just a theological treatise but a message about how to live, to work, to speak, to demonstrate faith. 13 lessons.

His Name Is Wonderful, Warren W. Wiersbe. Isaiah's power-packed descriptions of Christ have crucial and practical meaning for us today. A study of Christ in Isaiah. 13 sessions.

Leadership Life-style, Ajith Fernando. A clear examination of leadership training found in Paul's letters to Timothy. 13 sessions.

Listen! Jesus Is Praying, Warren W. Wiersbe. A verse-by-verse commentary on Christ's High Priestly Prayer in John 17 with practical applications. 13 sessions.

Live Up to Your Faith: Studies in Titus, Dr. James T. Draper, Jr. Christianity is more than right doctrines. Paul's message concerned both right believing and right living. 13 sessions.

Man Overboard, Sinclair B. Ferguson. A study of the life of Jonah. Not a story of a great fish but of a great God who deals with those who struggle with obedience. 6 sessions.

Master Theme of the Bible Part I: The Doctrine of the Lamb, J. Sidlow Baxter. An examination of the ten major passages from the Bible about the Lamb; a panorama of God's work of redemption. 13 sessions.

Proverbs: Practical Directions for Living, Dr. James T. Draper, Jr. A book to help people get a handle on the study of one of the Bible's most practical books. 13 sessions.

Run with the Winners, Warren W. Wiersbe. A study of Hebrews 11 and the "Hall of Fame of Faith." Defines biblical faith and how it works. 13 sessions.

What to Do Till the Lord Comes: Studies in 1 & 2 Thessalonians, Dr. James T. Draper, Jr. A relevant message to the church trying to remain faithful amidst opposition. 13 sessions.

DOCTRINE

The Apostles' Creed, J. I. Packer. A phrase-by-phrase explanation of the creed on which your faith in Christ rests. 6 sessions.

God in Three Persons, E. Calvin Beisner. The word trinity doesn't appear in the Bible, yet Christians hold it as a biblical truth. A study of how the doctrine was formulated. 6 sessions.

The Reality of Hell and the Goodness of God, Harold T. Bryson. A study of the biblical doctrine of hell and how it is consistent with a good and gracious God. 6 sessions.

Standing on the Rock: The Importance of Biblical Inerrancy, James Montgomery Boice. A study outlining the current controversy and the importance of accepting the Bible as inerrant. 6 sessions.

The Ten Commandments, J. I. Packer. God in love gave us not only the gospel but also the law. A study of God's moral absolutes. 6 sessions.

What the Faith Is All About, Elmer L. Towns. A layman's approach to Bible doctrine which provides the solid content for the development of believers. 52 sessions.

MARRIAGE AND FAMILY

The Family: God's Handiwork, John Williams. Put aside what psychologists and sociologists have said about the family and look at what the Bible itself has to say. 13 sessions.

The Family: Stronger After Crisis, Paul Welter. Conflict, anxiety, and depression become stepping stones for individual and family restoration and growth. 13 sessions.

Famous Couples of the Bible, Richard Strauss. A look at the marriages of the Bible shows how to strengthen your own. Good for a couples' class study. 13 sessions.

Hidden Art of Homemaking, Edith Schaeffer. Many opportunities for artistic expression can be found in ordinary, everyday life. How to make any home a center for meaningful living and personal enrichment. 13 sessions.

Marriage Is for Love, Richard Strauss. An insightful look at God's principles of happy marriage. A study to strengthen the fabric of your marriage. 13 sessions.

Parents, Take Charge!, Perry L. Draper. A psychologist explains important principles on child-rearing found in God's Word. 13 sessions.

Sex Roles and the Christian Family, W. Peter Blitchington. There is a specific pattern for family relationships designed by God and set in motion for our benefit. 13 sessions.

PERSONAL GROWTH/SELF-HELP

Discover Your Spiritual Gift and Use It, Rick Yohn. An examination of the relevancy and necessity of spiritual gifts in the life of every Christian. 13 sessions.

Dynamic Praying for Exciting Results, Russ Johnston with Maureen Rank. Christians have access to God's resources for life's demands. 13 sessions.

Handbook to Happiness, Charles R. Solomon. A professionally trained psychologist gives a Bible-based approach to solving contemporary personal crises. 13 sessions.

How Come It's Taking Me So Long: Lane Adams. A book to help new and growing Christians to understand the process of Christian growth. 13 sessions.

How to Get What You Pray For, Bill Austin. A study in how Christians can achieve greater success in prayer once they learn how to put themselves in harmony with the essential agents of prayer. 13 sessions.

How to Really Know the Will of God, Richard Strauss. Practical suggestions for decision making discovered in God's Word. 13 sessions.

Passport to the Bible, Bobi Hromas. Five minutes a day of Bible study and the Word of God comes alive. Bible study methods and dozens of ways to read, understand, and apply Bible truths. 13 sessions.

Self-Control, Russell Kelfer. A study of the enemies of self-control—the attitudes, appetites, and activities that threaten to control our lives. 13 sessions.

Spirit-Controlled Temperament, Tim LaHaye. A guide to understanding your God-given personality strengths and what the Holy Spirit can do to overcome your weaknesses. 13 sessions.

MINISTRY/PEOPLE-HELPING

Building People Through a Caring, Sharing Fellowship, Donald Bubna and Sarah Ricketts. Practical steps your church can take to develop koinonia fellowship and friendship evangelism. 13 sessions.

Effective Christian Ministry, Ronald W. Leigh. Principles of Christian influence based both on the Bible and on findings from the fields of psychology, sociology, and education. 13 sessions.

How to Help a Friend, Paul Welter. A study designed to teach Christians how to discover a friend's "living channels," and tips on expressing warmth, identifying needs, and responding to crises. 13 sessions.